Tr[...]ro: Roa[...]d Tips for Digit[...] Nomads and Frequent Travelers

Mish Slade

Contents

About the author

Mish and her husband Rob run a couple of businesses (copywriting and real estate) from their laptops while they travel the world. They blog about their experiences at www.makingitanywhere.com.

Introduction

Back in 2012, my husband Rob and I quit our London-based jobs and moved to New York for a six-month "sabbatical". The plan was to figure out what we wanted to do with our lives, then return to the UK to get on with doing it - probably freelancing or finding work in new companies.

Our friends and family already thought we were bonkers for leaping off the corporate ladder and creating a gigantic "VACATION!!!" gap in our respective résumés, so they were decidedly flabbergasted when - a few months after we'd arrived in NYC - we informed them of our decision to actually *set up our own business* and *do it while travelling the world.*

It's not hard to understand their confusion. Here we were - a young couple with a few lame "transferable" skills between us who really ought to be settling down and having babies - believing we could create a successful company out of nothing while living like (they assumed) gap year backpackers.

But we'd caught the bug, and there was nothing we could do about it. The bug wasn't the traditional "need to travel" kind - we weren't desperate to see every country, hike every mountain, ride elephants and catch overnight buses to bond with fellow travellers. We just realised that we wanted freedom - the freedom to do work we loved on our own terms, while living in exciting cities and getting to know and appreciate different cultures.

As soon as we began researching our dream lifestyle, we realised that we weren't exactly the spunky trailblazers we'd been high-fiving ourselves about: "digital nomadism", although relatively new, was slowly evolving into a huge movement consisting of people just like us - who wanted the opportunity and flexibility to see the world while making money by freelancing or running a business from wherever they happened to be. Thanks to the internet, this kind of life was now possible - and we all wanted to make the most of it.

The learning curve of building a location-independent business will need a separate book: this one's all about the travel aspect. When we started out in New York, we had two gigantic suitcases, zero knowledge of how to get the best deals on the best accommodation, a terrible track record with booking optimal flights, no clue about visas or insurance, and near-divorce experiences every time we approached an airport. How on earth were we going to move to a new country every couple of months without bankrupting ourselves, getting arrested for something we didn't realise we were doing wrong, or killing each other (which would also probably lead to arrest - but at least we'd know why)?

I'll tell you how: through trial, error and a fair few meltdowns.

Travel Like A Pro aims to save you from all that. Because although there were A LOT of laughs along the way, it was more like that hysterical cry-laughing that hurts and gives you hiccups. You don't need all that. You just need to know everything we've learnt so that you can get to where we are now: organised and efficient, and feeling free and happy about the lifestyle we've created for ourselves.

Who is this book for?

It's for people who have stuff to do, things to be getting on with, and no time to dilly-dally. If you're a digital nomad or you travel frequently or long-term, you'll find the tips in this book useful, expedient and quick-to-implement. That's what I'm aiming for, anyway.

None of the tips or strategies in here are about spending five hours clicking "refresh" to save $3, and they're not about selling your soul for upgrades. You won't find any suggestions about booking overnight trains in order to get a free night's sleep either. You love to travel but your life isn't about "hacking" travel. You simply want travel to be as easy as possible, so that you can get on with enjoying it.

Let's get started!

Mish

www.makingitanywhere.com

First off... get a free bonus chapter!

This book is about the planning and preparation part of travel. **If you'd also like to read about the process of settling into your new destination**, I've just written a 6,500-word bumper bonus chapter!

It includes information about:

- Your first steps as soon as you land

- Questions you mustn't forget to ask your Airbnb host

- Local transportation, and how to get to grips with it quickly and easily

- Finding and making friends with other digital nomads and frequent travellers

- Learning the language, figuring out the currency and understanding the customs

- Receiving mail

- Keeping fit when you don't have a regular gym or exercise class

- So much more - with HEAPS of tools and resources along the way!

To download it, just register your purchase of this book at www.protravel.co.

Chapter 1: Pack Like A Pro

No matter how much "stuff" you're currently lugging around with you, take comfort in this: we used to travel with a *microwave*. And a *kettle*. And 110 lb-worth of clothes, shoes, toiletries and electrical equipment.

This shameful baggage madness took place in NYC, where we'd just begun our digital nomad journey. We were spending six months living in 11 different apartments around the city (in order to experience as much of it as possible) - so every few weeks we'd pack everything into our mammoth suitcases (combined volume: 234 litres), our gargantuan plastic storage boxes and about seven humongous Kmart shopping bags, and then we'd hail a cab to drive us a mile to our next apartment.

We "needed" the microwave to reheat leftovers, and the kettle was a non-negotiable for two Brits who rely on "a nice cuppa" to calm down any situation. As for the clothes and shoes and toiletries and electrical equipment... we'd just unthinkingly packed everything when we left London, assuming that if we owned it, we needed it (even if "it" happened to be a bottle of bright red nail polish for nails that never *ever* got painted).

Soon we realised that we were taking the same items to the laundromat every week: most of our clothes weren't being worn. And *then* we noticed that we were wearing the same shoes pretty much every day. Not long after that, Rob pointed out that I hadn't used my hairdryer once because each of our Airbnb apartments already had one.

So we made a decision: from then on, every time we moved apartment we'd throw away or donate anything that hadn't been worn or used.

By the end of our time in New York we packed just ONE suitcase full of stuff, and the city's thrift stores had more stock than they knew what to do with.

We moved from New York to London to Thailand to Berlin, all the time whittling and whittling and whittling - down to what is now 20 lb of possessions each. Everything I own fits into a backpack, and the same goes for Rob. We're good for all seasons and - if this is your fear - we *never* have to sit by the radiator in our underpants waiting for clothes to dry before we can go out. Admittedly we can't attend a wedding, funeral or bar mitzvah at the drop of a hat, but it's always possible to go out and rent or buy occasion-appropriate clothing quickly.

If we were to turn back time to 2012, we'd do things differently. We wouldn't take all that stuff with us and gradually get rid of it all: we'd have the confidence to throw out pretty much *everything* before we headed off. And - if you haven't started travelling yet or you still need to go through bag drop at the airport - that's what I'd suggest you do too, as soon as you can.

If you're wondering if all the benefits are *actually* that great, they are! In the next section I'll explain why it's so wonderful to travel light. And after that, I'll help you figure out exactly what you need to pack for long-term travel.

The benefits of travelling light

There are many reasons why I think owning less and packing light is the way forward for anyone - but particularly for digital nomads and frequent travellers. Here are just a few of them:

Practical benefits

Minimal items —> carry-on baggage only —> ...

- Breezing through check-in? So much fun.

- Knowing that your suitcase can't go AWOL? A huge relief.

- Walking past the carousel that hasn't even *started* to move? Smugness overload.

- Beating everyone to the train station/taxi rank/bus stop? Even better.

- Walking easily up the stairs without gripping two hands to a suitcase handle and huffing as you drag it up step by step? Simply brilliant.

- Packing up your life's possessions approximately 15 minutes before you have to leave for the airport? Unbeatable.

Note: "travelling light" for me means travelling with carry-on baggage only. Your circumstances might mean that you *have* to put some items in the hold (you might carry lots of sports or photography gear with you, for example. Or you might prefer to give your kids real, hardback books to read).

And that's fine and completely understandable. You'll still gain a ton of "mental benefits" if you travel as light as you possibly can though, and the resources and tips in the rest of this chapter should still be relevant for you (except for, perhaps, the section on backpacks).

Mental benefits

We originally starting whittling down our stuff for the practical benefits, but we've since realised that the mental upsides are what *really* count...

We were never huge fans of shopping or accumulating "stuff", but becoming digital nomads has - to an extent through necessity - turned us even further away from that way of life. It's still fun to coo over the latest workout gear or wireless-enabled whojamaflip, but we also know what *really* makes us happy: experiences, relationships and meaningful work - not possessions.

We're not the only ones: multiple studies have shown that accumulating garages and cupboards full of stuff doesn't make anyone wildly ecstatic. In fact, the buzz of a new purchase wears off almost instantly, and all these possessions end up tying people down - and bringing them down in the process.

So... owning stuff doesn't make us happy. But does *not owning stuff* make us any *less* happy than we could be?

For example, are we consciously less happy when we make

salad in a saucepan because there aren't any large bowls in our Airbnb apartment? No, of course not. How about subconsciously? I really do doubt it. Or how about the fact that I have five t-shirts on constant rotation - would life be so much more amazing if I had 15 tops instead? I used to own far more than 15 t-shirts, and I can't remember having any "This is IT - the pinnacle of joy" moments of elation as a result.

But how do we feel when we're sitting with wonderful friends in some cosy little Eastern European cafe? Or checking out all the wildlife while walking up the Colorado mountains? Or even just waking up to a new view every few months? At times like those, we're so overwhelmed with happiness we feel like we could pop.

And then of course, there's the freedom that comes with having so few belongings. There's nothing quite like the feeling of travelling with your life's possessions on your back. You know you can go anywhere and do anything at a moment's notice. It's a *great* feeling, and once you know what it's like, you'll be hooked.

In the next section I'll run through some general principles to help you figure out what you need to take and how to pack more lightly. It's not an "overnight transformation": it might require a bit of a mindset shift first - and that's not easy. It took us *six months* to get down from two large suitcases to one, and another year or so before we were down to backpacks.

The principles of packing

These principles really helped us get to grips with what we really needed on our travels, and what we could do without:

- **Pack what you need, not "just in case".** You can't bring clothes and items for every possible situation, so just pack all the stuff you know you need during a regular week. If your best buddies suddenly decide to get married or there's a snowstorm in Hawaii, deal with it then by borrowing or buying. And remember: most "just in case" situations never happen.

- **If you're going to be moving between climates, you'll need clothes to suit them all.** You can always pick up an extra-thick jacket when you land in a cold country or buy a pair of flip-flops when you make an impromptu stop at the beach, but your general, basic everyday clothes should be good for all seasons. This means layers: t-shirts, warm tops/sweaters, leggings, jeans, etc. What you don't want is season-specific clothing: long-sleeved t-shirts are a bit of a waste in warm weather, and clompy leather boots won't get much use when it's boiling outside.

- **Invest in "performance clothing" - particularly for tops and sweaters.**
  Why, if you're not hiking or washing your clothes in

rock pools? Because performance clothing is made from fabrics (usually merino wool or synthetic fabrics) that are durable, lightweight, quick-drying and don't crease as much. They're also useful for moving across climates: the fabrics will keep you cool in hot weather and warm in cold climates. Aaaand they're great at wicking sweat away from your skin and keeping you smelling nice for longer.

Here are some great stores for performance clothing:

- **Backcountry:** www.protravel.co/backcountry (international shipping is available)

- **REI:** www.protravel.co/rei (international shipping is available)

- **Icebreaker:** www.protravel.co/icebreaker (international shipping to *some* countries is available)

- **Under Armour:** www.protravel.co/underarmour (international shipping is available)

- **ExOfficio:** www.protravel.co/exofficio (only ships to the US from its online store, but has international retailers - which can be found here: www.protravel.co/exofficio-locator)

- **Amazon:** www.protravel.co/amazon (lots of performance clothing stores also put their products on Amazon)

- **Wear your bulkiest items for travel.** I have some pretty hardcore (and heavy) walking shoes, so I wear them on the plane. My lighter shoes go in the backpack. Ditto my sweaters: I own a chunky, heavyweight one and a thinner, lightweight cardigan. The cardigan goes in the backpack.

  Women are luckier when it comes to jeans: there are many stretchy and lightweight ones available (I get mine from American Eagle). Men's jeans tend to be much bulkier, so if you're a man and you want to travel with a pair of jeans, try to wear them on travel days rather than pack them.

- **Make sure everything matches.** If everything goes with everything else, you'll have way more choice each day for what to wear. I know that even if *everything* except one top and one pair of trousers goes in the wash, I'll be fine because that top and those trousers will work well together. It's all about stripping down the colour palette and having a consistent style among all your clothes. (So, for example, don't have one really snazzy top if it'll only work with one pair of trousers.)

- **When it comes to toiletries, pack for the first couple of nights - and that's it.**
  Chances are, you're travelling to a city - a city that stocks headache pills, shampoo, soap and toothpaste. So just buy most stuff when you get there and take the bare minimum with you. Toiletries are HEAVY, so avoid taking too much in your carry-on baggage if you can.

- **Even if you can't find what you need in your destination city, you can always get it delivered.**

  Pro tip: If you're staying somewhere that can't receive mail or packages of any kind (like an apartment where you don't have access to the mailbox), you can use "Poste Restante" - a service where the post office holds mail until you go in to collect it. In the words of Wikipedia, it's a "common destination for mail for people who are visiting a particular location and have no need, or no way, of having mail delivered directly to their place of residence at the time." Visit the Wikipedia page for more information on how to use it in your particular country: www.protravel.co/post. And if your country isn't on the list, a bit of Googling should reveal everything you need to know.

- If you have a ton of stuff in a huge suitcase and you're

not quite ready to get rid of everything in one go, you can always do what we did: **every time you move to a new place, throw away or donate anything that hasn't been worn or used**. (And try not to worry about the "what if" scenarios when it comes to your ski boots or cocktail dress.)

Assuming you're on board with all this, let's get into the real nitty gritty: packing right, and then travel gear - what you need to know and what you ought to buy.

Packing right

Packing right starts with the bag itself. I'm a firm believer in the benefits of backpacks over any other type of baggage, and that's what I'll discuss first in this section. Then I'll move on to packing accessories (like packing cubes and toiletries bags) before finishing up with some super-cool gadgets and ingenious lightweight items.

Get a backpack

We've tried and tested a lot of bags over the years, and we now know what works best for us (and probably you, too): a backpack. Not a small roller, not a duffel bag, not a backpack with wheels. A backpack. One that fits into the overhead compartment, of course.

Here's why:

- Backpacks distribute weight more easily and are far more comfortable than duffel bags.

- Rollers are heavier, which means you're at an immediate disadvantage when flying airlines with very strict weight limits for carry-on (you can't carry so much of your own stuff because the bag is already so heavy).

- Rollers *look* bigger and heavier, which means you're more likely to get asked to check its weight/dimensions.

- Rollers don't squidge so easily into the metal frame if they're slightly larger than they should be.

- Even with identical dimensions, there's usually less space inside a roller or backpack with wheels, because the wheels and handle eat into the space available.

- Dragging a roller down the street is a hassle - particularly in Southeast Asian cities, but also in Europe where it's SO loud when the wheels roll along the sidewalk.

- A roller will take any opportunity to "roll over" the wrong way so that you have to stop, turn it around and continue on again.

- Stairs are annoying with rollers.

- There are more pockets/nooks and crannies to stash stuff in a backpack.

- With a backpack, both hands are free for water bottles, getting train tickets out, etc.

Not just any backpack is suitable though, and - as your choice of bag will play a very large part in your stress levels on travel days - it's worth doing a bit of research. You also might want to give your bank balance a bit of a heads-up - and a hand-on-heart promise that this expense *will* be worth it (and not at all like the time you paid for that gym membership).

What makes a good backpack?

Here's a checklist of some of the specs and features you might want to think about when researching backpacks:

- Is it advertised as being suitable as carry-on? (And do the dimensions match up? Ideally you want something that's about 22 x 16 x 8 in / 55 x 40 x 20 cm.) Remember: as backpacks are soft-sided, you can usually get away with slightly larger-than-ideal dimensions because the bag will still squish into the metal frame at airports.

- Is it large enough for your needs? (Don't feel like you should go super-duper minimalist just for the sake of it - if the bag fits the required dimensions for carry-on, that's all you have to worry about.)

- Is the material waterproof or at least water resistant?

- And are the zippers waterproof too? (Not essential, but definitely nice to have.)

- How easy will it be to pack your gear and find something inside the bag?

- Do other digital nomads/frequent travellers recommend it? What do they say about it?

- Can you imagine how all your gear will fit together neatly in the backpack? For example, where will your shoes go? And your contact lenses? What about your laptop - can it fit neatly inside without being crushed? Would you like a separate compartment for dirty laundry? Where can your passport and cash be safely stowed?

Next up: some recommended backpacks.

Highly recommended backpacks

For images of all these backpacks, head to **Appendix 2: Backpack photo gallery**.

Tom Bihn Aeronaut 45

This is what we own and adore.

It's a 45-litre backpack that fits the dimension requirements of most airlines. It has really useful side pockets, lots of nifty little hooks and key straps to attach items to, and it doesn't look like a traditional "backpacker" backpack. Instead it's sleek, smart and sophisticated, and - perhaps most importantly - *it looks smaller than it actually is,* which means we've never been asked to weigh it or check its dimensions at the airport.

Another huge benefit is that it's front-loading - like a regular roller suitcase - making it super easy to pack and a dream to find what you need (no more digging blindly down to the bottom to find the M&Ms that you're now desperately craving at the airport).

The most we've ever walked in one stretch with the bag has been about two miles, and it's been absolutely fine: no achey shoulders or feeling like we're going to fall backwards. We don't know when we'd ever be in a situation where we'd have to walk further than two miles (we'd just take public transportation or a cab), but it's worth bearing in mind that this isn't a hiking backpack, and it's not intended to be worn all day long.

If you'd like your backpack to double up as a hiking backpack, consider getting one with a metal frame - they're heavier, but they do an even better job of weight-distribution.

The Aeronaut costs $280 and it can *only* be bought from the Tom Bihn website (or in their Seattle factory showroom): www.protravel.co/tombihn. If you don't live in the US, shipping and handling costs about $30 extra.

Here are the key details:

- www.protravel.co/aeronaut

- Price: $280

- Dimensions: 22 x 14 x 9 in (55 x 35 x 23 cm)

- Volume: 45 litres

- Key features:

  - Front-loading

  - The main body of the bag is divided into three compartments via two zippered dividers: a large centre compartment that's flanked on both ends by pretty substantial end pockets. The end pockets can fit size-12 running shoes, dirty clothes, underwear, etc.

- If you don't want two end pockets, you can unzip one or both of them to have a larger main compartment.

- Padded carry handle at the top

- Reinforced, padded grab handles at either end

- Can buy a separate shoulder strap to carry as a shoulder bag

- Tie-down straps inside the main compartment

- Zippered side pockets for passports, boarding passes, etc.

- Waterproof coating and water-repellent zippers

Head to **Appendix 2** for pictures of this backpack.

Tortuga Carry-On Backpack

Tortuga is a relatively new brand focused almost entirely on the digital nomad market. The bags have dedicated laptop sleeves, and they look smart and businesslike. Although I love my Aeronaut, the Tortuga Carry-On Backpack is a serious contender - and one I'll definitely consider when I need to replace my current bag.

- www.protravel.co/tortuga

- Price: $199

- Dimensions: 22 x 14 x 9 in (56 x 36 x 23 cm)

- Volume: 44 litres

- Key features:

    - Front-loading

    - Quick-access front pocket for toiletries and anything you need during your flight

    - Laptop sleeve (fits laptops up to 17 inches)

    - Lockable zippers

    - Exterior pockets: two on the hip belt (for your passport, money or tickets); two on the sides for guidebooks, bottled water or electronics.

- Padded carry handles on the top and side

- Internal compression straps with pockets to stabilise your load and provide extra storage

- Exterior compression straps to condense your pack

Head to **Appendix 2** for pictures of this backpack.

Minaal Carry-On Bag

The Minaal team got their brand off the ground through a highly successful Kickstarter campaign, which they've used to build a loyal and dedicated following.

- www.protravel.co/minaal

- Price: $299

- Dimensions: 21.65 x 13.77 x 7.87 in (55 x 35 x 20 cm)

- Volume: 30 litres

- Key features:

    - Completely lie-flat packing

- Lockable side compartment containing a neoprene sleeve to protect your valuables

- Device compartments: main sleeve fits a 15" MacBook Pro with strap to hold smaller units safely; second sleeve fits a MacBook Air 11"

- Drink holder - holds bottles up to approx 3.54 in (9 cm) diameter - with adjustable cord

- Rain cover that packs into itself

Head to **Appendix 2** for pictures of this backpack.

REI Vagabond Tour 40 Pack

One of the original (and some still say the best) long-term travel backpack. The REI Vagabond Tour 40 might be considered more of a hybrid: its shoulder and hip straps are heavy-duty and make it suitable for hiking, yet it still looks decidedly un-gap-year-backpacker compared to many of the other bags on the market.

- www.protravel.co/rei40

- Price: $119

- Dimensions: 23.5 x 12 x 8 in (59 x 35 x 20 cm) - slightly

large, but easily squishable

- Volume: 36.5 litres

- Key features:

  - Shoulder harness and padded hip belt for carrying heavy loads

  - Zip-front panel provides wide-open access to contents

  - Top organiser pocket has a key clip and a pocket with a soft lining for phones, other tech and sunglasses

  - Side pocket can hold a water bottle

  - Inner compression sacks to maximise capacity

  - Outer lash patches let you attach extra items

  - Grab handles on the top and side

Head to **Appendix 2** for pictures of this backpack.

Useful packing accessories

It's easy to become overwhelmed by all the luggage accessories you can buy these days. From packing cubes and compression sacks to transparent pouches, money belts and organiser pouches… many of them do the same thing as each other, most are unnecessary, and combined they add a lot of unnecessary weight to your bag.

I've spent many years getting excited by all the accessories, buying them, and throwing them out. I'm now going to save you an awful lot of money and tell you exactly what you definitely need, plus a few optional extras:

The essentials

Packing cube and/or compression bag

Packing cubes and compression bags help to keep your clothes organised, neat and tidy.

Packing cubes are usually more like packing *cuboids*. They're extremely lightweight zippered fabric containers for your clothes that come in a range of dimensions, and you can use them in multiple configurations.

The key to saving space and saving on creases is to *roll* your clothes rather than fold them, and then pack them inside the cube.

Compression bags save space by forcing out most of the air inside the bag, which has the effect of compressing all the clothes inside it. Some compression bags require a vacuum nozzle for the air removal, but there are heaps on the market where you just "roll" the bag to squeeze out the air. Here's a video showing how a compression bag works: www.protravel.co/compressionvid.

With compression bags, rolling your clothes doesn't really work; instead you should fold them like you normally would, before rolling the bag itself to squeeze out the air.

So which should you go for?

We use just one packing cube each for all our clothes - the eBags medium packing cube: www.protravel.co/medcube. The dimensions of the cube work really well for us: the length takes up almost the entire width of our Tom Bihn Aeronaut 45s, but there's still a lot of space left over along the length of the Aeronaut for other items. (The packing cube doesn't take up the entire depth of our Aeronauts either, so we can easily fit our laptops and Kindles on top.)

Many people prefer compression bags - especially if they have more clothes than we do. (A popular bag is the Eagle Creek Compression Sac: www.protravel.co/egcompression.) I've tried them out but couldn't get on with them - I prefer to roll my clothes for a start. I also didn't like how the compression bags were often quite lumpy and bumpy - making it difficult to pack around them. Another reason is that the final shape of the compression bag seemed to be different each time I used it - so I'd have to figure out a way to configure all my *other* items differently whenever I packed.

However, there's no "best method": lots of people swear by compression bags. And many will combine the two - they might use a compression bag for their underwear or dirty laundry, for example.

Regardless of which you prefer the look of, get *something*: don't just put all your clothes straight into your backpack. Packing cubes and compression bags make everything so much more organised and easy to pack - and even the packing cubes will compress your clothes down to an extent.

Toiletries bag

Get a toiletries bag that will store the bare minimum. Remember: toiletries are HEAVY.

Many travel brands have created transparent toiletries bags for airport-security purposes, so you might like to choose one of those. There are plenty of options on Amazon, and this one from Flight 001 gets particularly good reviews: www.protravel.co/flight001.

You could of course just use a small Ziploc bag for all your toiletries instead.

Ziploc bags

Take a bunch of different-sized Ziplocs with you wherever you go - I swear they'll come in useful.

I use them for packing up food for the airport, storing toiletries, and for taking coffee granules with me in my carry-on bag so that I can make myself a cup of coffee when I arrive at my destination.

They can also be used as compression bags for underwear, clothes and dirty laundry.

And a ton of other things. They're mighty useful, cheap, lightweight, and hardly take up any space.

Shoe bag

My shoes came inside a fabric bag when I bought them, and I pack them in that bag when travelling. You could always use a plastic bag, of course. Just be sure to put the darn things in *something* - because there's nothing worse than mud all over your brand new backpack.

OK there are a lot of things worse. But I guarantee that the moment you see all the dirt and yuckiness, you won't thank me for pointing that out.

You can buy shoe bags really cheaply on Amazon. These ones are popular: www.protravel.co/shoebag.

Optional extras

Shoulder bag and/or laptop bag

If you're heading to the supermarket or a local cafe, you probably don't need 45 litres of storage space in your bag. So you might want to get a smaller bag for such occasions (unless you're able to fit everything inside your pockets - in which case, I'm jealous).

You can usually carry a shoulder bag in addition to your main backpack when catching a flight (see **Chapter 5: Survive The Airport** for more information), but nevertheless, try to get one as compact and lightweight as possible - just in case airlines change their rules or you decide you want to put it in your main backpack when travelling.

Here are some good options:

- **Tom Bihn's Packing Cube Shoulder Bag** (www.protravel.co/shoulderbag) is a nice way to combine two in one. I've had mine for two years and it's still going strong.

- **Eagle Creek's 2-in-1 Waistpack/Shoulder Bag** (www.protravel.co/waistpack) converts and expands from a waistpack to a shoulder bag and has a lockable main compartment.

- **Check out eBags for lots more**: www.protravel.co/ebags (Many of their products are also available on Amazon.)

If you're planning to take your laptop out and about at your destination though, you'll need a slightly bigger bag - but it still can't take up much space in your carry-on baggage! Here's what I do: I own the super-lightweight Sea to Summit Ultra-Sil Sling Bag (www.protravel.co/sling), which packs into its own teensy stuff sack and - when opened out - turns into a large shoulder bag that can bear weight of up to 280 lb (130 kg). It really is minuscule when all scrunched up inside its stuff sack - the length of my thumb.

The bag has no padding of course, but that's fine: my laptop is always protected inside its neoprene laptop sleeve. (Like this one on Amazon: www.protravel.co/laptopsleeve.)

Alternatively you could just use a regular linen shoulder bag, which is what Rob does. It also folds up really small.

Lots of other little bags and packets and dividers

You can pretty much store EVERYTHING inside its own little pocket or case if you want to - and you can spend days researching and comparing online. I don't tend to bother with anything other than my packing cube, toiletries bag, shoe bag, shoulder bag and laptop bag, but if you want to get excited by the unbelievable amount of packing gear that no one knew they *had to have* until they saw it, here are some sites for you to indulge in:

- **Eagle Creek**: www.protravel.co/eaglecreek (products are also available on Amazon)

- **Sea To Summit**: www.protravel.co/seatosummit (products are also available on Amazon)

- **Tom Bihn** (accessories page): www.protravel.co/tbaccessories

- **eBags** (accessories page): www.protravel.co/ebagsaccess

- **humangear**: www.protravel.co/humangear (products are also available on Amazon)

Now that we've covered the bags and containers you'll take, it's time to focus on the stuff you'll actually put inside them.

Small, light and ingenious items to carry with you

There are SO many amazing mini and lightweight products out there for travellers - many of which you'll want to buy even if you don't actually need them. Here are some of my favourites:

- **Lightweight insulated jacket: Rab Xenon X Hoodie** (www.protravel.co/rab). It's under 300g, rolls up into its own pocket, water-resistant, totally windproof, as warm as hell, and can be shoved in the washing machine. There are plenty of other lightweight insulated jackets out there, but I'd thoroughly recommend going for a *synthetic* one: the *down-filled* jackets are just as lightweight and just as warm, but they're not waterproof and can't be washed in the washing machine.

- **Small, lightweight camera: Panasonic Lumix LX7** (www.protravel.co/lumix). It has lots of manual functions and operates almost like a DSLR if you want it to, but it's far smaller and lighter. Plus, you can use it like a point-and-shoot if you'd prefer. (You could just use your smartphone's camera instead, if it's good enough.)

- **Sports shoes: Merrell Barefoot Flux Glove** (www.protravel.co/flux). These sports shoes mean that Rob no longer has use for socks in his life. They're extremely lightweight, and you can actually fold them in half when packing. Merrell is our favourite shoe brand, but there are plenty of other brands that do "barefoot" style shoes too.

- **Portable speaker: X-Mini Portable Capsule Speaker**
  (www.protravel.co/speaker). We've had this for four
  years now, and it's one of our best ever purchases. It
  means we can watch documentaries, talks, interviews
  and trashy telly on our laptops with fantastic sound.
  It's lightweight and super cheap.

- **MP3 player: SanDisk Sansa Clip 8GB**
  (www.protravel.co/mp3). Amazing, incredible, teeny
  tiny, reliable, a zillionth of the price of an iPod and
  just perfect in every way. (I don't use the MP3 player
  on my smartphone because I don't want to drain its
  battery, but plenty of people do of course just listen to
  podcasts and music on their phones.)

- **Cable lock: Pacsafe Retractasafe 250 4-Dial
  Retractable Cable Lock** (www.protravel.co/lock). I
  use this whenever we're travelling: I loop the cable
  through both our backpacks and then around
  something unmovable, like the storage rack above the
  seats on a train. If there's nothing that you can secure
  your backpack to, you can always just secure it to a
  friend or partner's backpack: someone is far less likely
  to be able to run off with them without you noticing.
  Also try to loop the cable through the zippers if you
  can.

- **SanDisk Ultra 64GB Memory Card:**
  (www.protravel.co/memory). We download a LOT of
  sitcoms, trashy TV shows, documentaries and
  interviews, so we shove them all on this to keep our
  internal hard drives free for work stuff.

- **Camera tripod: JOBY GorillaPod Flexible Camera
  Tripod** (www.protravel.co/gorilla). OK this thing is
  amazing: it's a very lightweight, bendable and flexible
  camera tripod that lets you attach your digital camera
  to *any* surface. We've been able to strap it around
  railings, onto door handles and balcony edges for
  fantastic, otherwise-impossible camera shots. The
  GorillaPod comes in a variety of sizes.

Where to find inspiration for other ingenious travel items

If - like me - you're the type to totally geek out over all this
travel gear, you might want to check out some of these
websites for inspiration and/or notifications when something
new and amazing comes on the market:

- **Kickstarter - technology category**
  (www.protravel.co/kickstarter). You might not be
  able to get your hands on any of the products you like
  until they've been successfully funded *and then*
  manufactured, but you get to be at the forefront of

something awesome and brand new.

- **Outgrow Me** (www.protravel.co/outgrow). Features Kickstarter products that *have* been successfully funded and are already available for sale.

- **Too Many Adapters** (www.protravel.co/tma). Great name, great site. Read all about the latest gadgets, travel gear and tips on everything from SIM cards to photo management.

- **Google** "digital nomad packing list [year]", "travel gadgets [year]", "travel tech [year]" etc. for up-to-date inspiration and ideas.

Conclusion

I have something to admit: my backpack weighs about 20 lb - which is already pretty light - and I know I could shave a few more lb off if I wanted to. But I like to travel with a big bag of jumbo oats. I'm a HUGE oatmeal fan, and I don't want to run the risk of landing somewhere, wanting oats, and not being able to find any immediately. I also carry measuring cups for the oats (because the world would end if I messed up my ratio of oats to water), and a fanny pack for when I go out running. I don't *need* any of these things; I want them. And they still fit into my carry-on, so I'm not bothered.

While I massively advocate lightweight travel and packing as little as you can get away with, you still need to be comfortable and confident, and you need to feel at home. What are *your* metaphorical comfort blankets - items you could live without but would really rather not? Figure out what they are, then find a way to pack them too.

Chapter 2: Book The Best Flights

Booking flights is a nerve-wracking process. Are you *definitely* booking the right dates, or are you a month (or a year) out by accident? Are these really the best prices available? Will the fare decrease by, like, $1,000 tomorrow and you won't be able to do anything about it? Have you chosen good seats? Are you sure this is the most convenient time to fly - should you go for the 2pm flight instead? Wait a minute! Did they just *trick* you into buying travel insurance, and a rental car, and - how did *that* happen - you booked an exit row and suddenly your fare has doubled in price? And... *no way!*...the destination "city" airport is one of those budget airline "city" airports that's actually a three-hour train, bus and cab ride away from the *actual* city! How'd you get yourself into *that* one?

The whole experience manages to be both terrifying and mind-numbingly boring in equal measure.

I definitely don't have it all sussed out, but I'm a lot more relaxed, organised and prepared than I used to be - and I'm able to grab hold of the best deals most of the time. In this chapter I'll go through some tricks I've learnt and tools I've discovered. And - towards the end - I'll also give you some ideas and inspiration for which destination to head to next.

I've also included a very small section on frequent flyer miles. The tips, tricks and deals surrounding frequent flyer miles change all the time, so I figured the easiest thing to do is provide you with links to some of the experts. These experts know everything there is to know at all times, and they make sure they constantly update their readers.

Once you've booked your flights and you want to know more about how to actually survive the airport/check-in/security/ boarding process, head on over to **Chapter 5: Survive The Airport**.

Find the best-value flights

While I've yet to find a failsafe five-minute strategy for getting the best-value flights, I *have* found an assortment of useful websites and tools that help me reach that goal. It's not the most elegant approach, but it works.

None of my methods involve stitching multiple flights together to reach your destination, or flying somewhere and then hiring a car to drive the final 200-odd miles. I figure you've got better things to do with your time.

Start with Skyscanner

Skyscanner (www.protravel.co/skyscanner) is a price-comparison and booking site for both domestic and international flights. It searches through "thousands of websites to find you the very best travel deals" across the majority of airlines, and presents them to you in price order.

When you find a deal you want, you can click to be connected to the airline or travel agent to make your booking directly with them. Skyscanner doesn't charge a fee for this (the airline or travel agent pays them a small referral fee instead), so you don't need to worry about paying extra.

There are lots of Skyscanner-esque sites out there, but I like this one because of the flexible search options: you can browse prices across an entire month or year, so - if your dates are flexible - you can make sure you're getting the best rates possible. It's also very user-friendly.

Here's what to do once you're on Skyscanner:

1.   Enter your starting city and destination, and search to find the best flights for you. **If your dates are flexible,**

look at the "month" or "year" view to see the best days to fly. (Alternatively, search for specific dates and once you're in the results page, click the right or left arrow to move up or down a day and see if the price changes.)

2. Once you're on the results screen, make a note of the best prices for the most suitable flights for you - and the airlines they're with. (You might be able to find a better deal out there if you do some more searching, which is why it's best not to book right away.)

If you're not a fan of Skyscanner or want to try something else, here are some other sites that aggregate airfares and allow you to book through them:

- Google Flights Explorer: www.protravel.co/gfe

- Kayak: www.protravel.co/kayak

- Hipmunk: www.protravel.co/hipmunk

Look up low-cost airlines separately

Southwest and Virgin America don't appear in Skyscanner's fare listings, and there are a few other airlines (like JetBlue) that don't appear on other aggregator sites. There might be a direct flight with one of those airlines, so check to see if that's the case.

Here's a Wikipedia list of all the low-cost airlines: www.protravel.co/lowcost.

And this site will give you a list of routes from low-cost airlines if you enter your starting location and final destination (Europe only): www.protravel.co/lowcostguide.

Check for hidden fees

We once booked a crack-of-dawn Ryanair flight from a middle-of-nowhere airport because we thought the fare was far cheaper than the airline offering the next best fare: British Airways. But after accounting for baggage fees (we had check-in bags at the time), the extra charge for reserving seats, and the time and cost of travelling to the middle-of-nowhere airport, we'd have been far better off going with BA (and we'd have had a lot more sleep).

Before you book anything, check for all the hidden fees! And if you value your time, make sure you account for that too.

- **SeatGuru (www.protravel.co/seatguru) has lists of all the baggage prices for each individual airline, as well as fees for checking in** - click on "Browse Airlines" at the top of the page. Bear in mind that SeatGuru's information is sometimes out of date, so you should check the airline's website too - once you've narrowed down your flight options.

- **Use Google Maps (www.protravel.co/gmaps) to see where the airport is in relation to your starting or destination city,** and - once the airport appears on the screen - use "Directions" to find out how long it'll take by different types of transit. If it turns out you can only get to the airport by taxi, Google "taxi fare calculator [name of city]": at least one website should appear in the search results to help you figure out an approximate price.

Check the airline's site directly for deals

Airlines often have deals that aren't advertised on price-comparison/aggregator sites, so - once you know what flights are available - you could quickly check the deals page of any relevant airlines to see if discounts are available.

Track flights for price drops

Yapta (www.protravel.co/yapta) is my hero website. It will track flight prices for you and alert you (by email, text, or through its iPhone app) whenever the price drops below a level you specify. You can then pounce as soon as the price is something you're comfortable with.

Don't stop once you've booked the flight! If the fare falls below what you paid for your ticket within 24 hours of your purchase, many airlines will refund you without penalty and allow you to rebook at the lower price. Use Yapta to track the flight you booked and alert you if it falls below what you paid. Yapta can then walk you through what to do to collect your refund. Find out more here: www.protravel.co/yaptarefunds.

Once your 24-hour window is up, Yapta can also email you if the airfare drops by more than the cost of the airline's change fee (the fee that kicks in for non-flexible tickets after 24 hours). You can then rebook at the lower price, pay the change fee and pocket the difference. More here: www.protravel.co/yaptarefunds.

If you have niche travel requirements...

If the price is right but you're *not quite ready* to book: use Options Away (www.protravel.co/optionsaway) to hold today's price for up to 14 days (for a small fee). If the airfare drops, you pay the lower price. If you decide not to travel, do nothing and let your hold expire. (At the moment, Options Away covers US domestic flights only.)

If you have a complex, multi-leg route: Orbitz (www.protravel.co/orbitz) is the most user-friendly when it comes to "multi-city" trips.

Extra tips

A few more tidbits of advice:

- **Try buying flights as if you're from another country.**
  For example, if you're American and you're flying
  from Sydney to Bangkok, search for prices on the
  Australian and Thai versions of the airline's site,
  rather than the US one: you can sometimes get better
  prices this way (but ensure that the charges levied on
  foreign currency transactions by your bank / credit
  card company doesn't screw up any savings).

- **Within 24 hours of booking a flight, check to see if
  the price has fallen.** If it has, you can usually get a
  full refund and rebook at the lower price. See the
  previous section of how you can use Yapta to track
  price changes on your behalf.

- **Waiting until the last minute to book is a risky
  move.** Most of the time, the fare will increase rapidly
  just before a flight, because it's filling up with other
  people and you're clearly desperate. On routes with
  significant competition though - like LA to New York
  - you might get lucky: some airlines will have sales if
  they're not selling enough seats quickly enough.

- It's probably best not to pay attention to a lot of the myths/no-longer-true situations about booking flights...

  - **Tuesday afternoon (or Wednesday morning, or Thursday evening) isn't the best time to search for flights, and the weekend isn't the worst time.** New fares are filed electronically - and they're filed throughout the day using a dedicated system that calculates how many seats are left on any given flight (unlike the old days when staff would manually enter new fares in batches).

  - **Websites aren't sneakily tracking how often you check a flight and upping the price because they can tell you're interested.** This myth was all over the internet a while back, and people were encouraged to use an incognito browser when viewing fares so that airline and flight-aggregator websites couldn't keep tabs on them. The myth was corroborated by the fact that people *would* often see two different fares for the same flight if they switched between their regular browser window and an incognito one.

    But as Hipmunk explains, "What might be

happening is that, if you get as far as the booking step for a ticket and it's the last seat at that price, the airline will put it 'on hold' until you've finished your purchase. So if you do another flight search immediately after, without releasing that seat, you might see tickets starting at the next price level." It's not in the interests of the website to raise the price, because you might go off looking for the cheaper price you'd seen earlier. (www.protravel.co/myth1)

- **You won't get the cheapest fare by booking a year - or even a few months - in advance.** As Bill Brunger, former vice president of Continental Airlines, explains, "[The airlines} don't know too much" a year out. "When revenue management people are nervous they usually pick a default level that's conservative." (Source: www.protravel.co/myth2) When *is* the best time? Well… it very much depends on the time of year and destination, so your best bet is to start tracking your flights ASAP (see the previous section on Yapta price alerts) and choose to buy when the price is something you're comfortable with.

If you're still keen on *some* kind of guidance for when to book flights... this Reddit thread shows the progression of ticket prices from two weeks to four months prior to departure date, and it suggests that between four and eight weeks before departure is a good time to book: www.protravel.co/whentobook1. And this study shows that prices start dropping at the three-month mark, with the cheapest tickets ranging from three weeks to ten weeks in advance: www.protravel.co/whentobook2.

Choose the best seats

Most airlines will allow you to choose your seats (although the low-cost airlines will often charge a fee for doing so). But beyond knowing whether you're an aisle kinda guy or a window-obsessed gal, how do you decide which part of the plane to pick?

(If you've never thought or worried about this before, ignore this section and go on as you were. There's no point in *adding* to your list of frustrations and worries when it comes to flying.)

SeatGuru (www.protravel.co/seatguru) is both your match made in heaven and your potential rabbit hole: there's just way too much fun to be had with airline-related information. SeatGuru has seating maps for all airlines, but where things get *really* cool is that the maps are colour-coded according to how good the seats are: some are considered superior according to the price you paid, while others are marked as downright awful and not worth a penny.

And who decides on the "colours" of the seats? Anyone - including you! The information is crowdsourced by users of the site. You'll also see a few written reviews of seats next to each plane's seating map.

(If you want to waste the rest of your day on airplane-related geekery, head to SeatGuru to compare all the airlines' first class cabins: www.protravel.co/firstclass. You can also browse SeatGuru's ever-fascinating blog: www.protravel.co/sgblog.)

Frequent flyer miles

In frequent flyer land, everything's constantly in flux. From the best deals to the best cards to the best hacks... it all changes practically daily. For that reason, it's way more useful to check out constantly updated websites on the matter rather than a book - so I'm providing you with some great links to get you started.

If you're a US resident...

If you're a US resident or have managed to apply for US credit cards, you're one of the lucky ones: frequent flyer miles are far more generous - and there's far more information about them - in the US than anywhere else in the world.

Getting started

- Start by reading this beginner's guide to miles and points from **Million Mile Secrets:** www.protravel.co/mms-guide. It's thoroughly comprehensive and will tell you everything you could possibly want to know.

If you'd like to do a bit more reading around the subject from a few different sources though, here are some other recommendations:

- Cards For Travel has a great step-by-step guide to understanding frequent flyer miles and getting started: www.protravel.co/cft-guide.

- You should also read this FAQ from them, because it's ace: www.protravel.co/cft-faq.

- Travis from Extra Pack of Peanuts has a comprehensive and thoroughly useful article called "How to use frequent flyer miles: the mega FAQ":

www.protravel.co/epp-faq.

- Also be sure to read his "Six myths of frequent flyer miles": www.protravel.co/epp-myths.

Finding the best deals

You only really need to check out one or two blogs for the best deals, because they'll usually tell you the same thing. Here are a few constantly updated sites:

- The Points Guy: www.protravel.co/tpg-deals

- Million Mile Secrets: www.protravel.co/mms-deals

- Extra Pack of Peanuts: www.protravel.co/epp-deals

You could also look at some forums. FlyerTalk is very popular: www.protravel.co/ft-deals.

If you're from the rest of the world...

Sorry to bunch you together with everyone else in the non-American world! It's just that there really isn't much in the way of information - because the perks are less widely available (and less good).

Take a quick look at the links in the previous section for US residents, because some of that information (especially the introductory guides) will still be relevant to you.

Here are some extra links to check out:

- If you're a UK resident, **MoneySavingExpert** is the place to go for a full explanation of how it all works, as well as up-to-date deals: www.protravel.co/mse-guide.

- If you're Australian, **Point Hacks** is a great resource for information and deals: www.protravel.co/pointhacks.

- Canadian? Head on over to **Rewards Canada** for step-by-step instructions to choosing a card, and links to the best deals: www.protravel.co/rewardscanada. There's also a great blog called Canadian Kilometers, which is all about frequent flyer miles (or kilometers) from a Canadian perspective: www.protravel.co/canadiankm.

There are also some great message boards and forums about frequent flyer programs. **FlyerTalk** comes highly recommended: www.protravel.co/ft-deals (scroll down to the bottom for discussions on European, Asian, Australian, etc. airlines).

Alternatives to flying

This chapter focuses mainly on flights because it's often the most efficient way of reaching a new destination. But for shorter trips (e.g. across Europe, within the USA or within certain other countries), it can make more sense to look into other forms of transportation.

Rather than list out all the different transportation options for all the different situations and countries, I'm just going to tell you about one seriously cool website. **It's called Rome2rio** (www.protravel.co/rome2rio), and if you're regularly doing short-haul trips or you're *really* fed up with gate announcements, there's a good chance you'll want to cuddle me after taking a look at it.

Rome2rio offers a "multi-modal, door-to-door travel search engine that returns itineraries for air, train, coach, ferry, mass transit and driving options to and from any location". Here are some use-cases:

- You want to know if you *have* to fly, or if you can go by train or car instead.

- You're visiting a ton of cities and towns across Europe, and you want a full itinerary including air, rail and driving options.

- You want directions to get from a specific address in

one country to a specific address in another (not just from, say, London to New York).

The site is pretty intuitive, but you can get some extra hints and tips here: www.protravel.co/rome2rio-faq.

Rome2rio isn't a booking site, but each journey contains links to sites that provide schedules and booking capabilities. These sites are either the relevant transportation provider (train operator, bus line, ferry service, etc.) or an online agency that specialises in that type of booking. **Wherever possible, try to book directly through the transportation provider rather than an agency to avoid unnecessary fees**. (These sites will almost always have an English language option, but if they don't you can use Google Chrome's built-in website translator or go to the Google Translate website (www.protravel.co/translate): copy and paste the URL of that website into the box.)

Tips on deciding where to go next

If you travel because you work online, or because you don't need to work, or because you take lots of "mini retirements" à la Tim Ferriss, you probably have a whole lotta freedom when it comes to your destinations.

And while it's AMAZING to have all that freedom, it can

occasionally be tricky to figure out where to go next. (Cue sarcastic comments from others about "hashtagfirstworldproblems", "nice problem to have" and "SUCH an awful life" - all of which are fair enough, and you should probably suck 'em all up gracefully.)

Here are some tips and resources that might help if you're struggling to decide where to go next:

- Use **Find A Nomad** (www.protravel.co/findanomad) to see where other digital nomads are hanging out around the world.

- Numbeo has a handy **cost-of-living comparison tool** (www.protravel.co/numbeo), which you can use to compare the prices of various products, food, accommodation, etc. of any two cities in the world - useful if you're budgeting.

- Use **Skyscanner** (www.protravel.co/skyscanner) **for inspiration**: in the "To" field, write "everywhere" (and in the "From" field, write the name of the city from which you'll be flying). Skyscanner will then present you with a list of destinations in price order.

- You can do the same using **Rome2rio** (www.protravel.co/rome2rio): type "direct flights" into the "TO" box and your city/airport of origin in the "FROM" box to show all the direct flights from that city/airport.

- **Nomad List** (www.protravel.co/nomadlist) is useful for giving you information about some of the top digital nomad cities in the world. There's data on cost of living, internet speed, air quality, temperature, and so on.

- If you enter your starting point into **Low Cost Airline Guide** (www.protravel.co/lowcostguide), it'll show you a list of destinations which you can reach with one direct, non-stop flight on a low-cost airline. The site includes airlines that don't feature in the search results of flight aggregator sites like Skyscanner.

Conclusion

Booking flights is a lot less tedious/terrifying for me these days, and it takes far less time than it used to. But there's no getting away from the fact that finding good deals on convenient flights requires a little bit of effort and persistence.

If you'd really rather not spend your time dealing with the ins and outs of airport locations, seat prices and frequent flyer miles, there's an alternative solution - something I've been thinking of trying out myself. You could hire a VA (virtual assistant) to do all the research and track all the flight prices on your behalf.

Start by sending your VA a list of all your requirements for *any* flight - e.g. you always want speedy boarding, you always want an aisle seat near the front, you'll travel between X and X time...).

Then send the VA a step-by-step process for finding the best-priced flights (you can adapt the tips in this book, if you like).

Then every time you need to book some flights, get your VA to do it!

You can find VAs on Elance, ODesk, or dedicated VA websites.

Chapter 3: Find Incredible Accommodation

This chapter focuses primarily on the "collaborative consumption" (or "sharing economy") model of finding places to live around the world - that is, renting other people's homes rather than staying in a hotel. From our experience, it's the most convenient and cost-efficient way to travel long-term. It's particularly useful for digital nomads who are trying to work while they travel, because being in a proper apartment (or house) usually means you'll have more room in which to organise your "work space" and "living space", and you don't have to go out to restaurants every time you want to eat.

There are many players in the collaborative consumption game, but Airbnb is the biggest and best - at least for the time being - so it's Airbnb that I concentrate on.

In some countries and in certain situations, it *does* make more sense to stay in a hotel or serviced apartment instead, so they're covered in this chapter too.

One thing I don't bother talking about is hostels: they're great for backpacking and meeting new people, but not so conducive to long-term travel, living like a local, or getting work done.

Let's get started...

Airbnb

Airbnb (www.protravel.co/airbnb) is essentially a marketplace that introduces "hosts" (people with a space to rent) to "guests" (people who need somewhere to stay). Airbnb doesn't own the properties, and no one from Airbnb itself has visited any of the properties to vet them. Instead, hosts and guests leave reviews for each other so you can be confident that you won't be ripped off. (Airbnb has also implemented a number of other "verifications" to make sure people are who they say they are.)

There are many benefits for guests:

- There are no bills to pay (gas, electric, etc.).

- There's no maintenance to do.

- You can simply pay your rent by PayPal (or credit/debit card, Google Wallet, Apple Pay…).

- Wifi, cutlery, crockery, sheets, towels, etc. are all provided.

- You're likely to have much more space than a hotel.

- If there are any problems (the property isn't up to scratch, the host is being an arse, you can't get in contact with your host for any reason…) you can contact Airbnb 24/7 for help.

And then of course there's the price:

- After accounting for all the bills, taxes, furniture, sheets, towels, cookware, etc. associated with long-term rentals, Airbnb can often end up cheaper (not to mention more flexible).

- And it almost (but clearly not quite) goes without saying that Airbnb is waaaaay cheaper than hotels. And you can compound that cheapness by doing your own laundry (rather than paying a hotel $2 per sock) and cooking meals (rather than eating out for every meal).

Some guests - including us - have taken things even further and are living Airbnb semi-permanently *instead* of having a home base. It gives us the flexibility to stay in a country/city as long as we want and move on whenever we get bored. It also removes a whole heap of hassle.

So with Airbnb you can move around the world while you enjoy the ultimate lifestyle flexibility.

COUPON ALERT! (If you haven't already signed up to Airbnb)

Use this link to sign up to Airbnb, and you'll get $25 credit added to your account automatically - which can be spent on any reservation that costs $75 or more: www.protravel.co/airbnb. Full disclosure: I'll also get $25 when you make your first booking, so we all win!

Before you get started... a quick Airbnb primer

In order to get the best deals and experiences out of Airbnb, you need to know a bit about how it works and how it differs from hotels or long-term rentals. Here are some key points:

- **All dealings happen directly between the host and the guest - Airbnb will only step in if something goes wrong.** (But be reassured that Airbnb really does help out if something goes wrong - it's not an empty gesture.)

- **While all communication happens directly between the host and the guest, payments do get processed through Airbnb.** As a guest, you'll pay Airbnb at the time of booking. Airbnb will only release that money to the host 24 hours *after* you've checked in, as long as you haven't reported any problems.

- In return for bringing both people together, processing payments and arbitrating if they need to, **Airbnb takes a small fee from both sides of the booking.**

- **There are two main types of listing:** individual rooms, where the guest and host share communal space; and entire properties, where the guest has exclusive use of the whole place. Individual rooms are cheaper, of course.

  There is a third option: "shared room", which means the guest shares a bedroom with someone else (as well as the communal areas), or the guest sleeps in the communal area itself. You won't normally find many of these on Airbnb.

- The main thing to remember is that **Airbnb is about personal interaction.** While on some listings you'll see the option to just book it right away using the "Instant book" button (instead of the "Request to book" button), most hosts like to know a little bit

about you before they decide whether to accept your
reservation request or not.

Which countries are "good Airbnb countries"?

Unless you're staying in certain parts of Southeast Asia, the
default place to look for accommodation should always be
Airbnb. We've stayed in apartments in Paris, Manhattan,
Brooklyn, Queens, Budapest, Prague, Berlin, London, Sofia,
Valencia, Madrid, Barcelona, Hong Kong and Bangkok, and
every single one of them has been ridiculously cheaper than a
hotel, more convenient (in terms of laundry, cooking, etc.), and
in some cases *extremely* high-end. We're talking infinity pools,
doormen, gyms, etc.

Soon we'll be off to Scandinavia. We may not be able to afford
a loaf of bread while we're there, but at least we can pay for the
roof over our heads.

The only reason to look outside of Airbnb in Southeast Asia is
because serviced apartments are a big deal in that part of the
world, and you might be able to find accommodation that
comes with daily cleaning, laundry service, room service, etc.
included in a very low rental price. Also, for some reason,
Airbnbs in Asia tend to be disproportionately expensive.

How long can you stay in an Airbnb?

There's no required minimum length of stay (although obviously you can't really stay somewhere for less than one night!), and the maximum length depends entirely on the host. To give an example, we've stayed in places for anything between two nights and four months.

You'll find that many (but by no means all) Airbnb hosts offer weekly and monthly discounted rates. You'll see these rates in the "Pricing" section of the listing description.

Tips for finding the best accommodation

Make use of the map on the search results page

The default classification of apartments into neighbourhoods/areas within a city might not be optimal for your needs. Here's an example of what happens when you search for an apartment in a specific location on Airbnb:

- Let's say you'd like to stay in the 3rd arrondissement in Paris. So you filter down your search results to that specific area within the city.

- Once the page refreshes, what you'll see on one side
  of the screen is a list of all the apartments that have
  been categorised as being in the 3rd arrondissement.
  The other side of the screen shows a map with pins
  denoting each of those apartments. What you *won't*
  see is any apartments that are *ever so slightly* over the
  border of that particular area.

The 3rd arrondissement is very expensive - and the Airbnbs
there are often overbooked (due to lots of tourists) and pricey
(because it's a highly sought-after area and hosts can raise the
price in line with demand).

The 11th arrondissement is less expensive and slightly less
"high end", but it's right next to the 3rd. On Airbnb, many
apartments are categorised as being in the 11th but they're
literally a few feet away from apartments that are categorised
as being in the 3rd. These properties are likely to be cheaper
because they aren't inside the tight boundaries of such a
desirable location and the host needs to keep prices lower to
attract demand.

So how do you find these apartments? Simple: use the map
view instead of scrolling through the list of apartments on the
other side of the screen!

All you have to do is move the map slightly into the less-
desirable location, and - if "Search When I Move the Map" is

ticked - you'll see lots of other apartments on the border that you otherwise wouldn't be aware of.

Look over Rob's shoulder as he finds a bargain apartment in an expensive area: register your purchase of this book at <u>www.protravel.co</u> for a free walkthrough video.

If you're struggling to find somewhere, remove all the "Amenities" you've selected

Here's the problem: for some reason, hosts go to all lengths to provide fabulous, imaginative and witty descriptions; they upload a gazillion photos of their beautiful properties... and then they don't bother to complete the "Amenities" section for the listing.

What does this mean for you? It means that if you selected some amenities, those properties won't appear in the search results - even if they have every amenity you could ever want.

If you're struggling to find somewhere suitable, you may as well remove any of the check boxes you've ticked and manually check if the resulting apartments meet your requirements. But if you're overloaded with options, leave the boxes ticked as a useful filter - just be aware that some listings will be filtered out when they shouldn't be.

Pay attention to the reviews

There are two distinct parts to the "Reviews" section: written reviews by guests, and star ratings for "Accuracy", "Cleanliness", "Check in", "Communication", "Location" and "Value".

Airbnb reviews are different from reviews on sites like Amazon, because the only people who can write them are those who've actually paid to stay. You can be quite sure they weren't written by other resentful hosts or family members who wanted to give the place a boost.

The host is also given the right to reply (on the page) to a review they deem unfair - meaning that when you read reviews, you should have a good idea of the property and the host.

The star ratings provide a decent overview (they're a sort-of average of the star ratings left by individual guests). But if the star ratings are low (below four stars for any category), be sure to read the reviews to find out why. A low "Location" rating might be because all other guests wanted to be in the thick of things, for example, whereas you know you'd rather be a bit more cut off from the hubbub.

Keep scrolling down the listings!

According to Airbnb, once search filters have been applied (like dates, number of guests, price, amenities and location), "listings are weighted by a host's aggregated activity on the site during the past 90 days. Activity during that time frame may include: a host's message response rate, the number of nights booked at the listing, the number of expired or declined reservation requests at the listing, and the number of host cancellations at the listing. Some of the host's activities beyond 90 days may also be weighted, such as the total number and rating of reviews and bookings a listing has received. The weights of each activity vary and are not disclosed."

All of this means that you should keep scrolling down your search results listings for some undiscovered gems! If a host is new to the site and hasn't received any reviews or accommodation requests, their place is unlikely to be near the top. So not only might you find something exceptional towards the end of your search results, but you might also get it at a lower rate because the host wants to get some good reviews on their page.

Use the "keyword" search if you have a specific concern/requirement

You can find the "keyword" search by clicking "More filters" on the search results page and scrolling down.

If you DEFINITELY want a kettle, for example, type "kettle" into the search box. You may miss out on plenty of places that *do* have kettles but don't mention it, but it's a quick way of getting the amenities you want without trawling through all the listings and looking at the photos and descriptions.

Note: the keywords filter only works on the property's title and description - it doesn't get applied to any of the reviews.

Make sure the apartment has everything you need

"Views shmews. Where are the fricking wall sockets?"

"I *suppose* I could take some of those books off the bookshelf, put them on the windowsill and make myself a desk that way?"

"I don't see where she keeps all the cutlery. Oh goodness, I *do* hope she has a decent vegetable knife."

"In-heaven alert, in-heaven alert! A padded headboard!"

This is what happens when you use Airbnb year-round rather than as a tourist: your priorities go doolally. All the things that normally matter to tourists (proximity to the sights, views from the window, etc.) take second place to a whole new weird set of must-haves.

Based on our experiences, here are some of those weird must-haves that you might want to look out for when going through the listings:

How many rooms?

As tourists, we never found it a problem to rent studio apartments: we were rarely in and we rarely cooked. Now, we really try to stick to one-bedroom places. If you're travelling on your own, this factor might be less important to you. But here's why we think one-bedroom apartments are preferable:

- If you're going to be working from the apartment too, it's nice to have a bit of a mental separation between "home" (the bedroom) and "work" (the living room/kitchen).

- Have you ever tried sleeping in the kitchen after you've prepared anything containing onions, fish, cabbage, or pretty much anything that isn't sandwiches?

- If you're travelling with a partner, you might just want a bit more space, and a bit more separation.

What size?

Our apartments have ranged from 200 square feet (19 square metres) to about 1,000 square feet (90 square metres). We now know that we're happiest when staying in places 450 square feet (40 square metres) or larger. It'll probably be different for you, but it's good to have an idea of the size you're happy with.

(If an Airbnb listing doesn't include the size of the place, just ask the host.)

Where are the wall sockets?

If the Airbnb photos show there are lights on bedside tables, you can be pretty sure you've got a couple of wall sockets there for charging up your phone and laptop. If there's a desk or sofa in the apartment, you ideally want a socket there, too.

We often go to work in a coffee shop after a stint working at home. And because coffee shops rarely have wall sockets, we need to be fully charged up while working from our apartment's bed, sofa or desk.

How much light is there?

This is something we didn't really care about when using Airbnb as tourists - because again, we were never there. But now we hate to be in a dark, dingy apartment while trying to work.

Many Airbnb apartments are photographed by Airbnb photographers - who overexpose the heck out of them. So it's important to read the reviews to find out what the apartment *really* looks like.

Another good indicator is the star rating for "Accuracy": if it's less than 3.5 stars, it probably means the photos are a poor representation of how the apartment looks in real life - usually a result of overexposed photos or furniture that's tattier than the photos imply. (Check the reviews to find out what the problem was.)

Is there heating or air conditioning?

Living in NYC in 100-degree heat is fine… if there's air conditioning to relieve you as soon as you're inside. And Prague's 20-degree winters aren't too much of a problem if you know you can get warm and cosy back at the apartment.

We've been surprised by the number of apartments that don't seem cut out for the perfectly predictable weather conditions of their respective cities. So now we make sure we find out what the temperature will be when we get there, and if the accommodation we're looking at has the appropriate heating or cooling system.

The "Amenities" section of Airbnb has "Heating" and "Air Conditioning" checkboxes that you can tick.

How will you do your laundry?

We have plenty of friends who just hand-wash everything, but we're lazy - and you might be too. A washing machine is pretty much a must-have for us (unless we're in a machine-free city like New York, where there are laundromats everywhere). So we always tick the "Washer" box in the "Amenities" section of Airbnb.

Is the cleaning equipment provided?

We're always scouring photos for evidence of items to clean with - vacuum cleaners, mops, bathroom sprays, etc. If we're staying somewhere a month, we want to be sure we can keep it clean!

If it isn't obvious in the photos, we'll often ask the host if cleaning equipment is provided - we're not going to shell out on a vacuum cleaner while we're there.

Is there a table of some sort?

In the olden days of "Airbnb for vacations", a table/desk wouldn't even come in our top 100 of nice-to-haves. These days though, a table of some sort is essential - for working, eating meals, and eating meals while watching *The Bachelor* on a laptop.

Is there enough space for your stuff?

If the host lives in the apartment when it isn't being rented out, there's a good chance the cupboards and drawers will be full of clothes. We've stayed in many places where we've had to lay our clothes across book shelves, or store them under the bed, or use the kitchen table as a wardrobe-cum-workspace-cum-dinner table.

It's not even like we have many clothes!

These days, we're more confident about asking the host in advance if there's any space for our clothes.

What's the cooking-utensil situation?

As a tourist, you probably couldn't give a fig whether there are enough cooking utensils, pots and pans in your apartment. But if you're travelling long-term and can't always be eating out in restaurants, it might be far more of a big deal to you. It's not make-or-break - you can always buy some - but it's far easier if you can move in and have a decent range of saucepans, bowls and cutlery.

Whatever kitchen equipment you end up with, be prepared for the fact that you won't find everything that you'd normally like to use - and a fair amount of imagination may need to go into your food prep. We now think nothing of serving a salad from a saucepan, or roasting chicken in a loaf tin. (Once, we didn't realise there were no sharp knives until after we'd done the shopping, so we "chopped" carrots with our teeth.) The key for us is to look for evidence of "enough" items, even if they're not the perfect fit for our cooking needs.

Oh, and a warning if you're British: get used to a lack of kettles. In Thailand, the US, Spain, France, Germany and Bulgaria we've had to boil water the old-fashioned way: in a saucepan on the stove.

What's the location like?

You'll have slightly different priorities from a vacationer when it comes to location. Here's what we look out for:

- We like to be within one mile of a largish supermarket, or else we can't be bothered to lug the bags home and we end up buying stuff from smaller, pricier stores nearby.

- We like to be within walking distance of at least one decent wifi cafe - so we can still get out and work when we're feeling particularly lazy and not in the mood to travel any further.

- We'd rather not be in the thick of tourist things. Everything's more expensive there, and the people are more annoying.

- However, we'd like easy access to the sights (via public transportation is fine).

- We don't need to be in the most happening place on the planet, but we'd like there to be a few nice restaurants and bars.

- If we're practically on top of a well-connected train or

bus station, we're very happy indeed.

Most importantly of all: what's the wifi like?!

OBVIOUSLY we tick the "Wireless internet" box on Airbnb. We also look out for a mention of it in the apartment description (just to be sure), and we scour the reviews for evidence of wifi playing up or being slow.

If you're particularly concerned, ask the host to do a speed test and send you the results. You can send them this link: www.protravel.co/wifispeed.

Tips on being accepted by the host

Many hosts naturally don't want just anyone with access to a PayPal account getting a set of keys to their front door, so there are many things you can do to ensure you give a good and trustworthy impression.

Below are the bullet points, but **if you want a bit more information on each individual tip (as well as some bonus tips), register your purchase of this book at www.protravel.co and you'll get access to all the advice you need.**

- Get a "Verified ID". Airbnb provides a lot of helpful information about this: www.protravel.co/verified.

- Have a profile photo and some profile information.

DON'T have a photo of a cute puppy or pretty
landscape.

- Get references from your friends.

- Send a nice, friendly message to the host.

- Don't ask to see the place.

- Don't ask to pay in cash.

- Send messages to lots of different hosts.

- Don't ask for a discount unless you have a great
  reason (such as a super-long stay).

Register your purchase of this book at www.protravel.co and
I'll send you extra information on all these tips, plus some
extra bonus tips.

Hotels

We prefer to stay in Airbnbs for the flexibility, the
independence (e.g. being able to cook our own meals) and the
feeling of really living like a local.

But you might be restricted to staying in hotels if there aren't
many Airbnbs in your area, or if you're visiting somewhere for
a short period of time and would rather just eat out every night

and have someone make your bed each morning. Or you might just want to go on vacation - which is when we tend to use hotels.

There are enough review sites in the world to help you figure out which is the *best* hotel for your needs, so I'm here to help with one thing only: finding good deals.

My favourite resources and strategies are coming up next, and they can often be used in conjunction with each other. None of my recommendations are dodgy or ethically dubious (I don't really feel comfortable suggesting that you pretend to be on honeymoon or a CNN news reporter), but I hope you'll still find a few of them fabulously sneaky - or at the very least quite novel.

Tip 1: Priceline's "Name Your Own Price"

With Priceline's "Name Your Own Price" (www.protravel.co/nyop), you bid for a certain class of hotel in a certain area. If your bid is successful, you find out which hotel you're staying in.

We saved 60% on our honeymoon hotels in Seattle and Vancouver using this: we got to stay in five-star hotels for a fraction of the price that everyone else was paying. The bidding process was more nerve-wracking than the wedding day itself, but it meant we could enjoy some full-on luxury that would otherwise have been out of our price range.

Extra tips:

- Use Better Bidding (www.protravel.co/betterbidding) to see the types of hotels that are often "won" on Priceline, along with the prices they were won at: it'll often help you narrow down the list of hotels you're going to end up with at the end of the bidding process.

- Bidding For Travel (www.protravel.co/ biddingfortravel) is similar to Better Bidding.

- Use Priceline's own "Real Hotel Winning Bids" along with Better Bidding or Bidding For Travel for an even better picture of the bidding landscape: www.protravel.co/winningbids.

- Be aware that if your bid is rejected, you have to wait 24 hours before you can make another bid. *However,* there's a workaround! Read the section on "How to get multiple bids" in this article: www.protravel.co/ workaround.

Tip 2: Hotwire's "Secret Hotels"

Hotwire (www.protravel.co/hotwire) is a bit less daunting than Priceline: it shows the room price, amenities and general location, but not the hotel's name. It's a great way for hotels to sell off excess capacity without aggravating their loyal and higher-paying customers (because they won't know that the hotel is secretly scooping up new guests for a much lower price).

Extra tips:

- Before you click to book any hotel, make sure you're saving as much as you think you are by researching the regular hotel prices for the area on the dates you'll be staying.

- If you want to at least *try* to discover the hotel's name before you book, there are plenty of tactics and resources at your disposal:

  - **Hotwire Revealed** (www.protravel.co/revealed)

  - **Better Bidding** (www.protravel.co/betterbidding)

  - **Bidding for Travel** (www.protravel.co/biddingfortravel)

- **Bid Goggles** (<u>www.protravel.co/</u><u>bidgoggles</u>)

- **Useful article on the Infinite Legroom website:** <u>www.protravel.co/predicthotel</u>

Tip 3: Hotels Combined

The Hotels Combined website (<u>www.protravel.co/</u><u>hotelscombined</u>) shows you the different prices for various room types across thousands of booking websites. It also aggregates reviews, star ratings, amenity lists and photos from those other sites, providing you with everything you might want to know.

There are other aggregator sites like Hotels Combined, but I think this one is the most user-friendly.

Extra tip:

- Once you've found a hotel that you like at a good price, take a look at the prices on the hotel's own website - they're often better. And if they're not, consider calling the hotel directly and asking for a better rate - you'd be surprised at how often they say yes. Even if you can't negotiate a better price, you can often get a couple of extra benefits like restaurant vouchers or a better room - just by asking nicely.

Even more tips on booking hotels

- On aggregator sites like Hotels Combined, you'll often see "**FREE cancellation, Pay later**" beside some of the rates listed. They're often no more expensive than the other prices listed, and they mean you won't have to shell out the cash until you arrive. Another benefit is that you can keep tabs on the price of your hotel room, and if it decreases significantly in the run-up to your trip, you can simply cancel and rebook at the lower price without any penalties.

- **If you'd rather leave the refunding and rebooking to someone else entirely**, try TripRebel (www.protravel.co/triprebel). If you book a (refundable) hotel room through them, they'll track your reservation for price reductions every day until you check in. If the price drops, you'll be automatically re-booked at the new rate and refunded the difference.

    TripRebel will also look out for new deals at superior hotels to the one you originally booked. Once they find something you might be interested in, they'll email you to see if you'd like them to change your booking.

    You don't have to pay a fee because the hotels pay TripRebel a commission every time a room is booked through them.

- Generally, you're better off booking hotel rooms sooner rather than later. Last-minute deals are best reserved for shorter, impromptu trips: you don't want to run the risk of being hotel-less for an important convention that you paid hundreds of dollars for. **The following apps specialise in last-minute deals:**

  - **Hotel Tonight** (www.protravel.co/ hoteltonight) provides "hand-selected hotels at great prices on your mobile device". You can book up to seven days in advance. The hotels are all top-quality and expensive, but significantly discounted compared to the regular room rates.

  - **Blink** (www.protravel.co/blink) is an app owned by Groupon. You can make a reservation for either tonight or tomorrow night, but no further ahead. By offering only truly last-minute rooms, Blink is often able to negotiate excellent discounts with hotels. The app is mainly for very short-term stays, but you'll be allowed to stay for longer than a night or two if there's space at the hotel.

- **The Suitest** (www.protravel.co/suitest) - US only for now - is a nifty little site if you want to **make sure**

you're getting a good deal on your hotel. You select your city, dates, amenities and so on like a regular hotel booking site, but there are a number of other features too - such as:

- "Suite Score" tells you at a glance how a room measures up to its peers by comparing the size, amenities, view and hotel quality of thousands of different room types in its database.

- "Fair Value Assessment" measures how much the room of a particular hotel *should* cost (compared to what it *does* cost) based on statistical analysis of the city, travel dates, neighbourhood, hotel quality, room size, amenities and view.

- "Price Graph" is a six-month calendar showing the average rate for each night in the city of your choosing.

- "Expose Fees" is a feature that adds fees for parking, wifi, taxes, etc. to the room prices so that you can see how much you'll really have to pay at the end.

- You have *far* more choice when it comes to which amenities you select. There's "double vanities", "large shower", "iPod docking" and loads more. You can even choose which type of flooring you want and what type of view you'd prefer.

- If you're interested in **general hotel gossip**, head to HotelChatter (www.protravel.co/chatter). It covers everything related to hotels and lodgings around the world, and you'll find stories about which celebrities are staying where, hotel industry news, tips for booking online, hotels to stay away from, and more.

- **Always book with a credit card**. Some hotels will place a "hold" on your card when you make a reservation - an extra amount on top of the regular cost of accommodation to cover for things like room service, breakages and overseas phone calls. The hold reduces the amount of available credit if you booked with a credit card, but actually reduces the *amount of money in your bank account* if you booked with a debit card. It will be released back to you after you check out, but there's a risk you'll be overdrawn (or with less cash than you anticipated) in the meantime.

- You can often **use frequent flyer miles to book hotel rooms** - and you can also earn frequent flyer miles when you book hotel rooms. There's more information on the following websites:

- Million Mile Secrets (for general information): www.protravel.co/mms-guide

- Points Hound: www.protravel.co/hound

- Rocket Miles: www.protravel.co/rocket

Serviced apartments

We've only ever used serviced apartments in Southeast Asia. They have all the benefits of Airbnb (independent living, a larger space than a hotel, etc.) with some additional extras - such as daily/weekly cleaning, a front desk to handle any problems, and extra amenities like a fitness centre and a pool. (These amenities can be found in Airbnb listings too, but not quite so frequently.) Serviced apartments are often cheaper than Airbnbs in that part of the world, so it's worth at least seeing what's available.

Finding good serviced apartments is a bit more of a random, trial-and-error process because there aren't any decent websites that aggregate all the information (like Airbnb or Priceline).

Here are some tips on where to look:

- **Google!** Type "[name of city] serviced apartments" and see what comes up.

- **TripAdvisor** (www.protravel.co/tripadvisor) has a section called "Specialty Lodging" for each city (you'll see it when you're in the "Hotels" section). Bear in mind that "Speciality Lodging" covers both hostels *and* serviced apartments, but if you filter down and specify that you want, say, a fitness centre, you're more likely to end up with list that's purely serviced apartments.

- **Hotels Combined** (www.protravel.co/hotelscombined) allows you to filter by "Property Type". If you tick "apartment", you'll see all the serviced apartments in the area - as well as prices from all the major booking websites.

- **Travel Fish** (www.protravel.co/fish) is a travel site dedicated to all things Asia. Head to the "Forum" section (www.protravel.co/fishforum), then type "serviced apartment [name of city]" into the search box (or just "apartment [name of city]" if you want more options). You'll find tips, ideas and relevant advertisements.

Once you've found a few possible options, contact the apartments themselves to see if they can offer better rates than those advertised on the websites.

Also bear in mind that most of these websites won't let you book for more than 31 nights anyway - so you'll have to contact the apartments if you want to stay longer.

Conclusion

Unlike the old days when we'd go abroad as tourists, accommodation can have quite a large impact on whether or not we enjoy our time in a particular city. If the wifi doesn't work properly or Rob and I can't hear ourselves think because of the noise outside, it affects our overall experience.

Before you start to look at the accommodation options in your next destination, it's worth putting together a list of your requirements - and then seeing how much you can match them when you scan through the listings. And don't make the same mistake we've made far too many times: letting a super-cool amenity sway you into staying somewhere you'd never normally consider. A shower with disco lights and water that pulses out in time to music does not make up for zero air conditioning in a sweltering apartment.

Chapter 4: Suss Out Insurance And Visas

Whoop - nitty-gritty admin time!

Insurance and visas are tricky to cover in a book aimed at more than one reader, because the advice and rules depend so much on the specific situation (country of citizenship, age, travel habits, etc.) of each person.

The other problem is that insurance options and visa rules are changing frequently, and it's hard to keep up!

In this chapter I aim to give you a good overview of all the things you need to think about, and links to constantly up-to-date sources.

Travel insurance

Think of travel insurance as cover for emergencies - for situations when your bags get stolen, you have to cancel your trip at the last moment, or you get eaten by a panda. Travel insurance is essentially for the big bad stuff that's unlikely to happen but might.

With that said, let's move on to what it actually includes...

What's included?

Here are the four main types of situation you're covered for, with guidance on how to ensure you actually get a payout:

- **Emergency medical treatment.** This usually covers you for all forms of emergency medical treatment and repatriation to your home country by air ambulance. Remember that this covers EMERGENCIES - it isn't a replacement for your normal healthcare or health insurance, and it won't cover you for general checkups, minor illnesses, non-critical operations, etc.

  After reading *a lot* around the subject, I've concluded that the minimum cover you should look for is $3,000,000 (which includes repatriation).

  Make yourself a bucketful of coffee and read the fine

print though: there's a lot of it, and you need to know about all the exceptions. If you're planning on doing any crazy-ass sporting activities or you have any pre-existing medical conditions, read everything twice.

- **Trip cancellation/curtailment.** If you need to cancel your trip or cut it short due to a personal or family medical emergency, your insurer will refund or part-refund you for any of your non-refundable travel costs like flights and accommodation. There's always heaps of fine print though, so make sure you read it all.

  When it comes to the minimum amount you should be covered for, it should be based on whatever you think is reasonable for the cost of your trip.

- **Luggage loss or theft.** You'll want to be covered for whatever you think your luggage is worth, and then you'll be reimbursed for all or part of its value if any items are lost, stolen or damaged. Beware of many, many things though:

  - There's usually a single-item limit on contents of luggage - often about $500. Unless you're *amazing* at haggling with Apple or Amazon, your electronics are probably worth a whole lot more than that - so you might want to consider taking out extra insurance on them (I'll come to this later).

- When you claim, you'll often need to prove you owned the items in the first place - so be sure to take photos of your receipts and then store them digitally. To be on the safe side, you could also take photos of the products, and mark down information about the brand, style and so on in a spreadsheet.

- If you fail to report stolen property to the police within 24 hours of discovery, you won't get a pay-out (usually).

- Big bit of "urrrrgggghhhh" coming up... you'll usually be offered the value of your belongings *minus* depreciation - so you won't be able to purchase a brand new version of an item that was lost or stolen with the insurance money alone. Want to read more about how depreciation is calculated? Course you do - it'll put you in a lovely mood! Here's a great article on the topic: www.protravel.co/depreciation.

- **Personal liability.** This shouldn't be confused with any motoring claim you may need to make; if you've hired a moped or car, you should take out a separate policy. Personal liability claims are there to cover you if you damage or break anything, or if you injure someone.

Ideally, you should be covered for at least $1,500,000.

Don't forget about the deductible!

Most travel insurance plans have a "deductible" - an amount you're required to contribute towards your expenses when making a claim. (It's also known as an "excess".)

Do you definitely need travel insurance?

There's a chance your credit card company already has you covered for lost luggage and/or cancellation, so you may not even need travel insurance for those purposes.

Even if your credit card company *doesn't* cover you, you might think that travel insurance isn't worth the expense for lost luggage or cancellation: there are just so many provisos and ways for insurance companies to wriggle out of paying you.

The BIG decision though, is whether you need (or want to bother with) the medical part of travel insurance.

Here are some things to think about before you decide:

- **You need to pay close attention to what you're covered for when it comes to medical treatment.** Usually, you're covered for all forms of emergency medical treatment (existing health conditions excepted), and you're also covered for repatriation to your home country by air ambulance. BUT once you're in your home country, you're on your own. If you don't have health insurance or free healthcare there, travel insurance might become a whole lot less valuable. (This isn't to say you *shouldn't* get travel insurance - just that you need to think about what happens if you're repatriated after an accident.)

- **If you're a legal resident of a European Economic Area (EEA) country or Switzerland, you can get the European Health Insurance Card (EHIC) for free:** it entitles you to free or reduced-cost medical treatment in those European Economic Area countries and Switzerland. You're also covered for pre-existing medical conditions and routine maternity care.

  You might decide that the EHIC is enough if you're travelling within Europe, but be aware that you won't be covered for any private medical healthcare or your return journey if you need to come home. Also - because each country's healthcare system varies - your EHIC may not cover all costs (or you may have to pay to "top up" certain treatments). You should also bear in mind that you're not covered for the non-medical aspects of travel insurance, like cancellation or lost belongings.

You can read more about the EHIC here: www.protravel.co/ehic.

- If you already have health insurance in your home country, **you** *might* **already be covered for basic care if you have a medical emergency when abroad**. You won't be covered for repatriation though, and you'll usually have to pay out of pocket before being reimbursed by the health insurance provider (whereas with travel insurance, the hospital will often be able to talk directly to the travel insurance provider).

If you ask me (let's assume you did), travel insurance is worth it for medical emergencies if nothing else - even when taking into account the points above. You (or someone you know) can call a 24-hour helpline as soon as you're in the ambulance and confirm that you're covered for whatever treatment is necessary. Usually, the hospital will be able to take over from there and arrange all funding for your treatment directly with the insurer (unless it's a small cost - in which case you may be asked to pay and then get reimbursed by the insurer later). This is particularly useful if you're in a country where healthcare is expensive: if you have a medical emergency and no travel insurance, your bills are going to be through the roof.

Think you're fit and healthy and that nothing ever goes wrong? Even if you have the world's healthiest heart and milk-supplemented bones of steel (I have no idea what I'm talking about), your appendix could throw the hugest tantrum TOMORROW - the very day, in fact, that a flesh-eating parasite could take a sudden fancy to your elbow.

Medical emergencies happen to healthy people too - that's all I'm saying.

Three very important caveats to all travel insurance policies...

Pay close attention!

- You're not covered for pre-existing conditions (unless you find a specialist insurer).

- **You're not covered for regular health checkups or non-emergency treatment.**

- Outpatient treatment is covered in certain circumstances, but most of the travel insurance providers recommend that it's easier to pay for this out of your own pocket than claim on insurance.

Think of travel insurance as "emergency insurance" - it's not supposed to replace your normal healthcare.

Types of travel insurance (and providers)

If you've decided that you *do* want to go ahead and get travel insurance, read on…

There are three main types of "traditional" travel insurance:

- **Single trip:** one trip, usually lasting no more than 31 days. (You can choose between "European", "Worldwide excl. USA, Canada & Caribbean" and "Worldwide", which all have different prices.)

- **Annual multi-trip:** multiple trips throughout the year, each one lasting no more than 31 days. (You can choose between "European", "Worldwide excl. USA, Canada & Caribbean" and "Worldwide", which all have different prices.)

- **Backpacker:** a whole range of countries on one extended trip. (Policies vary, but you can get backpacker insurance for up to 18 months.)

If you regularly make short trips abroad, annual multi-trip insurance may well be all you need. To find the best deal, **use Google's** *excellent* **travel insurance comparison site to find**

the best provider for you: www.protravel.co/googleinsurance.

If you're always travelling around rather than returning "home" - or you tend to stay for long stretches in one place - the above insurance options (including annual multi-trip) aren't so useful for you:

- You need to be in your home country at the time of purchasing the insurance.

- When you take out the insurance, you usually need to specify a return date (or at the very least, your insurance will expire after a certain number of months and you'll have to return home).

- You can't renew the insurance while on the move.

Luckily, more and more travel insurance options are coming onto the market for people who travel long-term and have no return date - meaning you often *don't* need to be in your home country at the time of purchasing the insurance, you *don't* need to specify a return date, and you *can* renew the insurance while on the move.

Here are a few companies that come highly recommended; check them all out because some might be more reasonably priced than others depending on where you're from and where you're travelling:

- **World Nomads (www.protravel.co/worldnomads) is a firm favourite among digital nomads.** The staff are known to be very friendly and helpful on the phone, and they're also great at answering questions on Twitter (@WorldNomads). They provide a lot of coverage and - according to many - will process claims quickly and fairly rather than try to find ways to get out of them.

- **Worldwide Insure offers "Longstay Travel Insurance"** (www.protravel.co/worldinsure) for EU residents. Areas of travel can be mixed to suit your needs, and you can extend the travel insurance any number of times while you're still travelling.

- **World Escapade** (www.protravel.co/escapade) gives you the option to *just* have medical coverage and none of the other stuff (like cancellation and baggage coverage), which is a great idea.

Expat health insurance

Think of expat health insurance as your replacement for the regular healthcare you get (or used to get) in your home country. If you're American, think of it as health insurance. If you're British, think of it as the NHS or private healthcare.

Whereas travel insurance covers you for medical emergencies, expat health insurance is there for your dental check-ups, your earache, your flu-like symptoms and - with certain provisos - your pregnancy.

You don't just have to live in one country as an expat - you can buy insurance that will cover you for medical attention all over the world.

What's included?

Here's the lowdown:

- **It's usually renewable for life** - which means that if you're on a particular expat health insurance plan and develop a disease or chronic illness, you should still be able to renew your policy when the time comes (they won't just kick you out because you're suddenly more expensive to insure). And you won't have to pay a honking big premium at renewal time either.

- **You can often use your expat health insurance back home, too.** So if you're American and have expat health insurance that covers the US, you'll be able to use it there. (Be sure to refer to what your policy states in relation to "home country coverage" first though.)

- Most insurance providers give you the option to **get covered for some or all of the following (as well as**

some or all *within* **the following)**. The more you pick, the higher your premium will be:

- **In-patient:** treatment received in a hospital where an overnight stay is necessary. Cover includes things like hospital accommodation, anaesthesia and theatre charges, surgical fees and diagnostic tests.

- **Out-patient:** treatment provided in the practice or surgery of a medical practitioner, therapist or specialist (where hospital admission isn't required).

- **Maternity:** medical costs incurred during pregnancy and childbirth, midwife fees, hospital charges, specialist fees, etc. (Normally, you'll need to be with the insurance company for a certain amount of time before they'll offer you maternity cover.)

- **Dental:** check-ups, fillings and root canals as well as more complex procedures like gum disease treatment and orthodontics.

- **Well-being:** e.g. an annual well-being checkup.

- **Vaccination:** immunisation and booster injections as well as pre-vaccination consultations.

  (Thanks to the website Broker Fish for help with the above list.)

- Some insurers will cover chronic conditions too.

- You can *sometimes* get cover for pre-existing conditions (although your premium will increase).

Which is the best expat health insurance provider?

Aaaaah the 64-thousand-dollar-in-deductibles question!

The answer depends on so many things: your age, what you want to get covered for, where you're going, and so on. Rather than trawl through all the different health insurance sites though, just head to **Broker Fish** (www.protravel.co/brokerfish).

It's pretty nifty: it allows you to compare all the expat health insurance plans easily, and you have lots of options for filtering down your results. For example, you can choose what types of cover you want (dental, out-patient, well-being, etc.), how much you want your deductible to be (the higher the deductible, the lower the monthly premium - and vice versa), where in the world you want to be covered, and so on.

There's no charge for using Broker Fish: the company receives commission from any insurer it places cover with instead. And because there's relatively little variation in the amount that Broker Fish receives by plan or insurer, there's no reason for them to recommend one over another to you.

Do you definitely need expat health insurance?

It depends.

- Do you have national healthcare or private health insurance in your home country - and do you return there frequently? You may not need expat health insurance if you think you can fit in all your doctor's appointments and checkups on your trips back.

- Are you going to be living in countries that have extremely cheap, "on demand" private healthcare, like Thailand? It might be cheaper *not* to get expat health insurance and just shell out as and when you need to. (Or at least, you might decide to risk *not* buying expat health insurance because you know that any medical care won't be inordinately expensive.)

Remember: **you don't have to have continuous, year-round expat health insurance if you don't want to.** We went to NYC for six months and decided to purchase health insurance for that trip, but otherwise we don't tend to bother because we're relatively healthy, and because we return to the UK (where we can use the NHS and do the rounds at the physician, dentist and eye doctor) every three or so months anyway.

Insurance for your high-value items

Your travel insurance plan will cover you for the loss, damage or theft of your belongings, but you're usually only insured for quite a stingy amount, and there's a limit on how much you can claim for a single item - around $500.

When it comes to buying "gadget insurance" or "high-value items" insurance, there are very few insurers who'll cover your gear while you travel the world.

Here are some options, but I'm afraid none of them is perfect:

- **Protect Your Bubble** (www.protravel.co/bubble) will insure your smartphone, tablet, camera, laptop… all of it, for a low monthly fee. The drawback is that you only get worldwide coverage for up to 180 days a year. (Also, your country of residence has to be the

UK, US or Australia.)

- **Photoguard** (www.protravel.co/guard) offers worldwide cover for photography equipment... but only for UK residents.

- **AppleCare** (www.protravel.co/applecare) is essentially an extended warranty plan for your Apple products, and it's AMAZING for people who travel: you get two or three years (depending on the product) of totally free repairs - parts and labour included - from any Apple store or Apple-authorised service provider around the world. You can either take your damaged product into the store or mail it to them. You also get free phone-based tech support.

  Another benefit of having Apple products over other brands is that most Apple stores will carry the parts needed to repair your product - so it can be done right away. When Rob's Asus laptop broke recently while we were in Valencia, the computer repair store had to wait ten days for a part to arrive before it could be fixed. It's the same with a lot of other brands: there aren't always dedicated stores, so you have to wait ages to get the product fixed (and it costs a fortune to do so).

  AppleCare is the main reason why I switched from a

PC to a Mac last year. It's not cheap, but for me it's totally worth the peace of mind - especially as pretty much every city we've lived in has an Apple store.

The cost of AppleCare depends on which products you want to take it out on, but for some guidance it's $249 at the time of writing for a MacBook Air (that covers you for the full three years). You can find out the latest prices here: www.protravel.co/appleprices. Be sure to check the benefits you get for each type of product because there *are* small differences.

So what makes AppleCare anything less than perfect? It isn't really an insurance plan, so it doesn't cover theft. And I've been told that not *all* Apple stores around the world carry *all* parts (especially in Southeast Asia), so you may occasionally have to wait a while.

Visas

A visa is essentially a permit to visit another country. Sometimes you won't need a visa at all, sometimes you'll *definitely* need one, and sometimes your particular travel circumstances will dictate whether you need one or not. It all depends on where you're travelling from, where you're travelling to, why you're travelling there and how long you plan to stay.

I'm not an immigration expert but I've been to a lot of countries, read a crazy amount of information and heard lots of stories from friends. However, please be sure to do some extra visa-related research whenever you travel to a new country - especially as I can only give you a general overview rather than any specifics.

Here goes…

Visas for short business trips

If you frequently travel on business, you're unlikely to be in a country for a significant amount of time, so you just need to use VisaHQ (www.protravel.co/visahq) to figure out if you need a business visa and - if so - how to go about getting one.

Visas for digital nomads/ perpetual travellers

We digital nomads are in a bit of a grey area when it comes to visas - the main reason being that the reality of being able to work online has overtaken the rules that govern international work.

Working visas are intended for people who are working for employers (and potentially taking jobs away from locals) in the

area, and business visas are for those who are there purely to
further their business in some way. Digital nomads don't fall
into either category, so the majority of us tend to imagine
ourselves as tourists - because there aren't really any other
options for us.

What does this mean in practice?

- If tourists need a visa to enter a particular country
  (e.g. Thailand, if staying longer than 30 days), digital
  nomads will get a tourist visa - and if any border
  officials ask, they're there for a vacation.

- If tourists don't need a visa to enter a particular
  country (e.g. Hong Kong), digital nomads won't get
  any sort of visa.

You can use VisaHQ to find out if tourist visas are required for
the country you're planning to visit: www.protravel.co/visahq.

How to get a visa

Assuming you're taking the "I'm a tourist" approach to visas,
you just need to follow the visa rules for tourists.

Use Visa HQ (www.protravel.co/visahq) to find out if you
need a tourist visa or not, then just do a bit of Googling to
discover whether you can get a visa on arrival or if you should
order one in advance. (If you're required to get a visa in

advance, you'll need to send off your passport to the relevant embassy and wait a while - so try to get on top of it as soon as possible!)

In some countries, you're allowed to renew your tourist visa at least once while you're still in the country. In other countries, you have to leave and come back again. Google "visa run [country]" for more information and advice.

Do you need a visa for your layover?

If you're flying into one country's airport simply to fly straight out to another destination, you may still need a visa for that intermediary country - even if you don't ever leave the airport. The rules vary widely, so you'll need to do some Googling: search for "transit visa [country of layover]" and some useful results should appear.

Even if you don't need a visa, you can't stay forever!

While many countries will let you into the country visa-free, there's still usually a maximum number of days you can stay in that country. For example, if you're American you'll be allowed into Germany without a visa… but you're allowed there for a maximum of 90 days out of every 180 days.

If you want to stay longer than your allowance, you may have to apply for some sort of visa or residency - it will depend on where you're going.

Occasionally there are nifty workarounds - especially when it comes to living in Europe. If you're not European and you want to stay there for longer than 90 days, Nomadic Matt has some ideas on how to achieve it: www.protravel.co/90days.

Conclusion

It took me forever to get to grips with visas and insurance: I never knew where to start looking for information about a particular country or specific situation. Now that I've done the research though, it's a doddle - and I hope this chapter has given you more confidence in getting to grips with your own visa and insurance situation.

It's still admin, but it's a far more straightforward and less convoluted, flail-about-in-the-dark kind of admin.

Chapter 5: Survive The Airport

It was after seeing the movie *Up In The Air* that I realised plane travel *can* be a breeze.

In the (yes, OK, entirely fictional) movie, George Clooney is a MASTER frequent flyer: he glides through check-in, dances through security, and never waits anxiously by the gate-announcement board before dashing like a madman to be first to get on the plane and secure the overhead compartment directly above his seat.

I'll admit that while we aren't quite at Clooney-like levels of suaveness and sophistication when it comes to plane travel, we've come a long way. We get through security quicker than you can say "Is that really a 2 lb bag of rolled oats in her backpack?", we no longer need to panic that our precious carry-on will be removed from us as we try to board the plane, and we know *exactly* where we're going (and how to get there) when we land.

How have we achieved this? It's taken years to figure it all out, but we think it comes down to these three things:

1.   Pack light

2.   Know the rules

3.   Stay organised

Let's go through each of them in turn.

1: Pack light

The practical and mental benefits of packing light should not be underestimated - which is why there's a whole chapter dedicated to the subject (**Chapter 1: Pack Like A Pro**). And it's at airports and on airplanes that the benefits are most immediately noticeable. When nothing needs to go in the hold and all your stuff can fit into the overhead compartment, these wonderful things happen:

*   You can sail past those huge lines at check-in/bag drop and head straight for security.

*   You don't have to pay unnecessary baggage fees (on

budget airlines).

•   You don't need to panic that your life's possessions
     have accidentally been rerouted to Azerbaijan.

•   You get to experience the immense, intense,
     unmatchable pleasure of gliding past the bag carousel
     while everyone else sits waiting for the darn thing to
     get started.

If you want ideas and tips for *how* to pack light, head back to
Chapter 1: Pack Like A Pro.

2: Know the rules for carry-on baggage

As I'm British, here's what I'll say about the rules relating to air
travel: they're somewhat confusing, occasionally a little bit
silly, perhaps a tad excessive and at times a jot frustrating.

If you're a frequent flyer, these rules aren't cute little
idiosyncrasies - like humongous Toblerone bars and 8am
vodka tonics - that mark the start of a vacation; they're the
bane of your life. Airline rules trip you up at security, make
things difficult as you're boarding, and get you all antsy and
distracted when you're trying to relax in the departure area.

To master the rules, you need to be aware of what they are…

Rule #1: Carry-on baggage size and weight

Airlines - the low-cost ones in particular - are becoming increasingly tetchy when it comes to carry-on baggage allowances. So if you don't want your life's possessions taken from you and shoved in the hold (where they'll be brutally knocked about and have a small chance of going to the wrong destination), you need to be aware of the rules - and how to cleverly overcome them.

Before you fly, it's your job to be aware of the maximum **bag dimensions**, the maximum **weight of your bag**, and the maximum **number of items** you can take with you on the flight.

(If you already have a good idea what the rules *are*, skip on ahead to the "How to navigate rule #1" section of this chapter.)

Maximum bag dimensions

These vary according to airline (although not half as much as they blimmin' vary when it comes to weight limits - which I'll come to). Here are a few examples for economy class; the dimensions always include handles and wheels:

- Ryanair: 22 x 16 x 8 in (55 x 40 x 20 cm)

- Virgin Atlantic: 22 x 14 x 9 in (56 x 36 x 23 cm)

- American Airlines: 22 x 14 x 9 in (56 x 36 x 23cm)

- British Airways: 22 x 18 x 10 in (56 x 45 x 25 cm)

- Virgin America: "maximum outer linear dimension of 50 inches [127 cm]" - e.g. 24 x 16 x 10 in (60 x 40 x 25 cm)

- Thai Airways: 22 x 18 x 10 in (56 x 45 x 25 cm)

- Cathay Pacific: 22 x 14 x 9 in (56 x 36 x 23 cm)

- Southwest: 24 x 16 x 10 in (60 x 40 x 25 cm)

- Easyjet has a "cabin bag guarantee", which means that if your bag is up to 19 x 16 x 8 in (50 x 40 x 20 cm), it will definitely be allowed on the plane with you. If your bag is up to 22 x 18 x 10 in (56 x 45 x 25 cm), it's still "allowable" as carry-on but may be taken off you and put in the hold if it's a busy flight.

To find out the most up-to-date dimensions for your airline (they change frequently), just Google "[name of airline] carry-on". SeatGuru also lists the baggage allowances for all airlines: www.protravel.co/sgbaggage.

Carry-on weight limits

Weight limits are all over the place.

For example…

- Easyjet: no weight limit (the only stipulation is that you have to be able to put the bag into the overhead compartment by yourself)

- Ryanair: 22 lb (10 kg)

- British Airways: 51 lb (23 kg) ?!

- Virgin Atlantic: 22 lb (10 kg)

- Thai Airways: 15 lb (7 kg)

- Cathay Pacific: 15 lb (7 kg)

- Southwest: No weight limit specified

(All weight limits are for economy class.)

To find out the most up-to-date baggage weight allowances for your airline (they change frequently), just Google "[name of airline] carry-on". SeatGuru also lists the baggage allowances for all airlines: www.protravel.co/sgbaggage.

Number of items you can take on the flight

When you travel, you can no longer take one large item of carry-on plus a coat, a handbag, a laptop case, a separate toiletries case, an umbrella, a sandwich, a magazine, a neck pillow and a massive teddy bear: the airlines all got wise to that trick.

At the time of writing, Easyjet is the biggest meanie in this category: you're allowed just ONE piece of carry-on - whether it be a backpack, handbag, laptop case or carrier bag. The only other items you're allowed to carry in addition to your one cabin bag are: overcoat, shawl, umbrella, crutches and one standard size bag of duty free from the departure airport.

Most other airlines are slightly more lenient: you're usually allowed a handbag or laptop case in addition to your one piece of carry-on baggage. Again, to find out the most up-to-date rules for your airline, Google "[name of airline] carry-on" or use SeatGuru: www.protravel.co/sgbaggage.

How to navigate rule #1

Use a backpack for your carry-on

In **Chapter 1: Pack Like A Pro**, I mentioned that I was a huge fan of the Aeronaut 45 by Tom Bihn (www.protravel.co/aeronaut). Although it ever so slightly exceeds the maximum dimensions for some airlines (it's 22 x 14 x 9 in / 55 x 35 x 23 cm), it's soft-sided - so unless you've *really* stuffed it full, you'll be able to squish it into that terrifying metal bag-testing frame at the gate.

Tom Bihn products aren't cheap - and other decent, hardwearing backpacks are also quite pricey. But I do think backpacks rather than rollers are the way to go. As a reminder why:

- Rollers are heavier, which means you're at an immediate disadvantage when flying airlines with very strict weight limits for carry-on (you can't carry so much of your own stuff because the bag is already so heavy).

- Rollers *look* bigger and heavier, which means you're more likely to get asked to check its weight/ dimensions.

- Rollers don't squidge so easily into the metal frame if they're slightly larger than they should be.

Get smart with the maximum number of items you can take on a flight

With most airlines, you shouldn't have a problem when it comes to the maximum number of items you can take on a flight: you're usually allowed one large piece of carry-on plus a smaller bag like a handbag or laptop bag. That seems fair and reasonable: one item to go in the overhead compartment, and a smaller bag (for your food, Kindle, etc.) that can fit under the seat in front of you.

But Easyjet is different: you're only allowed ONE piece of carry-on, maximum. (You can take a coat or a shawl or an umbrella, but no other bags.) And other airlines might decide to follow suit in future.

So here are some ways to deal with it:

- **Buy duty free at the airport.** On Easyjet flights you're allowed one bag of duty free in addition to your one piece of carry-on. So if you're up for being a bit sneaky, buy something small and cheap in duty free, and ask for a large plastic bag at the checkout. Then put your handbag into the duty free bag before you arrive at the gate.

- **Get a jacket or coat with super-large pockets, and stuff your belongings into them.** Skyscanner has reviewed a selection of "wearable baggage" jackets - head to www.protravel.co/wearable to view them. You'll look ridiculous, but there's a reason this book isn't called *How to Look Hot and Score Dates at Airports*.

- **Pack a small, lightweight shoulder bag in your carry-on.** I own the super-lightweight Sea to Summit Ultra-Sil Sling Bag (www.protravel.co/sling), which packs into its own teensy stuff sack and - when opened out - turns into a large shoulder bag. I can pack this into my backpack and then - as soon as I'm on the plane - open it out and stash my Kindle, food, water, etc. inside it for the journey, storing it under my seat while putting my main backpack in the overhead compartment. The bag doubles up as a laptop bag when I'm at my destination (it has no padding, but my laptop is always stored in a neoprene laptop sleeve).

Something to bear in mind: airports have their own policies when it comes to the number of bags any person can take through security as carry-on. These policies are usually more generous than individual airline policies, so they shouldn't trip you up, but it's wise to check the airport website before you travel - just in case.

Board the plane ASAP

There's always* the risk that - no matter how small your carry-on - the overhead compartments will all be stuffed full by the time you board, and you'll be forced to put your own bag in the hold.

(*Apart from with Easyjet, which guarantees that if your bag is no larger than 19 x 16 x 8 in (50 x 40 x 20 cm), it will definitely be allowed on board with you.)

This scenario is actually far more preferable to checking your bags in the first place: at least you know your bag is definitely going in the hold of *your* airplane. However, it's still not ideal to have your life's possessions taken away from you - so here are some tactics we use to optimise our chances of getting our bags on the plane with us:

For short-distance and/or budget flights:

- **Get to the gate PRONTO.** You usually won't get called to the gate until it's time to board - and then it's a case of first come, first served to get on the plane. To avoid being last in line, rush to your gate AS SOON as it's announced! Extra tip: find an information desk in the departure area and ask them for the gate number. They'll often give it to you before it's announced, meaning you'll have extra time to get to the gate before everyone else.

- **Consider Speedy/Priority Boarding.** Many low-cost airlines offer Speedy Boarding or a similarly named equivalent for a small fee, allowing you to be first onto the plane. Bear in mind that you'll still need to get to the gate in good time: boarding occurs very shortly after the gate is announced, so if you're late to the gate there's a good chance the "regular" line will have started boarding. You'll still be allowed to push in because of your Speedy Boarding, but that's no use if you're one of the last ones to arrive at the gate.

With many low-cost airlines, you don't board the plane
through the jet bridge but have to pile into buses to get to the
plane instead. There are normally a couple of buses to any
airplane, so your job is to get on the *first* bus - meaning you'll
still need to be at the gate in good time!

For long-distance and/or non-budget flights:

Other passengers are more likely to put all their gear in the
hold (because they'll probably be travelling for longer and
haven't learnt how to pack ninja-light) - and as a result they'll
take up less space with carry-on. But you still want to up your
chances of being one of the first on the plane… just in case.

So…

- **Find out the boarding pattern for your particular
  airline.** SeatGuru has all the information you need:
  www.protravel.co/boardingpattern. Then select your
  seats based on which ones are allowed to board first.

Rule #2: Liquids and sharp objects in carry-on baggage

In 2006, terrorists plotted to detonate liquid explosives on
board at least ten airplanes travelling from the UK to the US
and Canada. They were foiled before anything happened, but
the "no liquids in carry-on baggage" rule remains in place

throughout most of the world.

Different countries have slightly different policies when it comes to liquids in carry-on, but the general gist is this:

- Liquids may only be carried in containers holding 3.4 oz (100 ml) or less.

- They must be carried separately in a single bag (one bag per passenger). The bag must be:

    - Transparent and resealable

    - No larger than 8 x 8 in (20 x 20 cm)

    - Able to close properly with all the items inside

- You need to place the bag in the tray with your other items at security.

- Liquids include:

    - Bottled drinks

    - Suntan lotion

    - Fragrances

- Cosmetics

- Toiletries

- Contact lens solution

- Baby food or baby milk is allowed in quantities larger than 3.4 oz (100 ml), as long as you're actually travelling with a baby. (If you're on your own, don't think you can get away with "But Jen Aniston *swears* by the baby food diet…")

- You can carry liquid medication in excess of 3.4 oz (100 ml) only if it's needed during the course of your flight. All medication needs to be accompanied by documentary proof of authenticity, like a prescription or letter from a medical practitioner confirming that you need it for your journey. Liquid medication that isn't required on the flight will need to go in the hold.

As for sharp or dangerous objects, here's what you need to know:

- You can take insulin and needles with you on the plane, as long as you have the documentary proof of authenticity described above.

- When it comes to knives, razor blades and scissors, the rules can differ quite significantly from airport to airport - so be sure to check your own before you travel. Sometimes you'll be asked to remove your nail scissors; other times you'll be OK if the blades are less than a certain length. I had my eyebrow tweezers taken away from me once, but I'm just going to assume the airport employee was having a bad day that day.

- Martial arts equipment and blunt sports equipment like baseball bats and batons aren't allowed in carry-on.

- I'm not going to list all the guns, incapacitating devices, power tools or poisonous/explosive substances you're not allowed on the plane with. If you're thinking of travelling with a slingshot or a crowbar, you're not the sort of person I imagined would read this book.

These rules only apply as you're going through security; once you're in the departure area you're free to buy liquids, scissors, etc. in the shops there.

Remember: check the website of your departure airport for specific rules and regulations.

How to navigate rule #2

There are some pretty easy workarounds/solutions/money-saving tips to deal with the rules on liquids and sharp objects in carry-on baggage…

- Take an empty plastic water bottle with you to the airport, and fill it up at a fountain (usually found near the toilets) once you're through security. Bottles of water tend to cost a fortune at airports, so this is a good way to avoid the otherwise-inevitable "Yowza, $9 for an Evian????" freakout.

  (Warning: a few airports will have an extra security point right before the gate - so you may have to throw out your water again! You can usually find out by Googling "[name of airport] security screening boarding gate".)

- Buy travel-sized shampoo and conditioner bottles, and reuse them every time you travel (just refill them from the regular bottles that you buy at your next destination).

- Take an individually wrapped bar of soap in your bag: it'll last longer than a small bottle of shower gel, and you don't have to try to squeeze it into your 8 x 8 in (20 x 20 cm) baggie along with all the other liquids.

- Use nail clippers instead of scissors.

- Use stick deodorant (which doesn't count as a liquid)

instead of spray, gel or roll-on deodorant - which will all need to be in containers no larger than 3.4 oz (100 ml) and placed in the baggie.

- Buy a travel-sized tube of toothpaste.

- Don't bother with face wash, cleanser, etc. Take face wipes if you have to, but otherwise just use soap and water the first night and make your way to a supermarket or pharmacy the following day.

There are tons and tons of non-liquid alternatives to most toiletries, but they can be quite hard to find in certain locations - and they're often not as good or easy to use as the liquid version.

Rule #3: Electronic items in carry-on

You can carry laptops, MP3 players, Kindles, tablets, smartphones and so on in your carry-on. But you should be aware of a few extra rules and guidelines before you travel with them:

- At security, you'll be asked to remove "large electrical items" from cabin baggage and protective sleeves. "Large" usually means where any dimension is greater than 8 in (20 cm) in length, such as a laptop.

Smaller items like e-readers and tablets can usually remain in cabin baggage and protective sleeves, but it might be easier to just whip 'em out too (as some Kindles and e-readers seem to set off the machines anyway).

- Make sure ALL your electronic items are charged before you travel. In certain countries you might be asked to switch on your device, and if you can't (because the batteries are dead), you won't be allowed to take it on the flight - and there's a good chance you won't be allowed on the flight either. Turning on an electronic device can show a security screener that the batteries aren't in fact hidden explosives.

Rule #4: You (sometimes) need proof of onward travel

When you arrive in a new country, the border officials there may want to see evidence of your travel arrangements to exit the country too. (See **Chapter 4: Suss Out Insurance And Visas** for more information on how there's almost always a time limit for staying in a country.) It's called "proof of onward travel".

"Proof of onward travel" might be a round-trip plane ticket, a plane ticket to another destination, or another kind of transportation ticket (bus, train, ferry, etc.) to another country.

If you don't have proof, you might be denied entry into the country. As a result, some airlines have taken it upon themselves to *refuse to board passengers* who could be denied entry to their destination. Why? Because the airline may have to return you back to where you came from, at their own expense. And they'd really rather not risk it.

The ridiculous part is just how ad-hoc the whole system is...

- Sometimes a country doesn't require proof of onward travel, but the airline staff might still throw a wobbly because they're not aware of that and they're just trying to stay on the safe side.

- Many countries *say* they require proof of onward travel, but they never seem to ask for it - and the airline doesn't seem to care either way.

If you're doing frequent yet short business trips, you probably have a return ticket. But if you're bouncing around from one country to the next, it's likely that - even if you're not planning on overstaying your welcome in one country - you don't yet know where you'll be going next.

If this is you, you have a few options:

- **Take the risk and hope no one catches you without**

proof of onward travel. Many people do it and get away with it just fine.

- **Buy a cheap plane, train, bus, etc. ticket onto another country nearby**. A potential problem here is that the border officials won't want to risk you being turned away at the *next* border. I haven't heard of anyone who's had this issue, but it's mentioned on travel blog posts as something to think about.

- **Buy a plane ticket back to your home country**. If you get a ticket back to your home country, the border officials can be fully confident that you'll be allowed back in.

    If your home country is a very long way from your destination, you could get a fully refundable one. Bear in mind that fully refundable plane tickets are bloomin' expensive, and you might have to pay off your credit card before you're able to apply for the refund (putting you out of pocket for a little while).

- **Buy a fully refundable ticket only when you're prevented from boarding**. It's a risky move because the plane won't hang around and wait for you to figure out your own shenanigans. But it's been done before…

- **Get organised and figure out your itinerary a few**

months in advance. Boring, but you often get the additional benefits of: cheaper flights, cheaper accommodation, and lots of build-up excitement.

If you're travelling to Europe...

If you're not European and you're travelling to a country that's inside the Schengen Area, your proof of onward travel must be to a country that's *outside* the Schengen Area.

(The Schengen Area comprises 26 European countries that have abolished passport and any other type of border control at their internal borders. For your purposes as a non-European, it pretty much counts as ONE country, and you're allowed to stay up to three months out of every six without a visa. You can live in as many Schengen-Area countries as you like within those three months, but you have to leave completely once three months are up. If you're from a European country that isn't part of the Schengen Area - like the UK - you still have free movement within the Schengen Area.)

3: Stay organised

"Staying organised" isn't just about arriving at the airport on time and having your passport with you. If you want to be a travel ninja (and avoid all the fluster and panic that goes with *not* being one) read on...

- **Set a calendar reminder to check in online.** Some airlines allow you to check in up to a month before your flight - which seems insane but there you go. Other airlines will allow you to check in 24 hours before your flight. And certain flights don't really "do" check in anymore. For example, when you buy certain tickets with Vueling, you automatically check in at the same time.

- **Check in online.** If you don't already check in online, you're a) missing a trick and b) errr... insane?? Checking in online means the following:

  - You don't have to check in at the airport, which is SO much quicker (especially if you're travelling with carry-on only and can proceed straight to security).

  - Most of the time, you can get your boarding pass sent to your smartphone after you've checked in online - meaning you don't have to locate an internet cafe to print it out before the flight (and it's one less thing to remember to take to the airport).

  - With some airlines, you can only actually choose your seats during the check-in process (not before). If you wait until you reach the airport to check in, you might have missed out on all the best seats.

- And remember: certain airlines ONLY allow you to check in online!

- **Assume you'll be caught in a traffic jam** (or insane train delays) on your way to the airport - i.e. leave for the airport *really* early! It's better for your nerves, and you can use the extra time at the airport to listen to podcasts, read a book, or do some work.

- **Always have *one* place where you keep your passport and boarding pass** (if it isn't an electronic one), so that you always know where they are. They should be easy to retrieve at the airport, because you'll need to pull them out every five bloomin' seconds.

- **Wear clothes that don't need a belt.** Wear shoes that can be slipped on and off easily. And if at all possible, pack your jacket in your carry-on. It all leads to less hassle in the security line.

- **Put your liquids, laptop and other electronic devices in a place that's really easy to reach within your bag.** Again - for ease at security.

- **Make sure your laptop and other electronic items are fully charged.** (See carry-on baggage rule #3 for more information.)

- **Buy a retractable cable lock for your bag.** While you're in the departure area, use it to lock the zippers together and then tie the bag to a permanent structure. I use the Pacsafe lock, which is available on Amazon: www.protravel.co/lock. Plenty of other brands do them too.

- **Take an empty water bottle with you through security**, so that you don't have to pay the always-exorbitant price for a bottle of water in the departure area.

- **Have enough cash with you to buy anything you might need at the airport.** Some airports (I'm looking at you, Sofia-Vrazhdebna Airport) don't have ATMs, and their stores don't take cards.

- **Take food with you for the flight.** It's cheaper, healthier and tastier. You're allowed to take your own food through security, unless it's in liquid form (like yoghurt) - then it's subject to the same rules as other liquids in your carry-on baggage (see carry-on baggage rule #2 in this chapter).

  (Bear in mind that for some reason you're NOT allowed to take outside food onboard an AirAsia flight. But everyone does anyway, and no one seems to get into trouble for it.)

- As mentioned earlier, **listen/look out for your gate announcement** and don't dilly-dally when you hear / see it. And consider buying a Speedy Boarding ticket for low-cost airlines. Essentially, you want to be on the plane putting your bag in its overhead compartment ASAP.

- **Keep a pen handy for writing out your landing card/ customs form** on the plane.

- **Store the address of your final destination (as well as any other useful contact details) in your phone**, OFFLINE. I keep all the info in Google Keep (www.protravel.co/keep). That way, even if something goes wrong with my phone data - or if I don't *have* any data yet - I have all the info I need when we land at the destination airport. (Google Keep syncs all your notes across all your devices, but it's always available offline too. You can also use Evernote (www.protravel.co/evernote), but I find Evernote a bit too cumbersome and unnecessary for short little notes like this one.)

- **Figure out how to get from the airport to your destination in advance.** If it's a train, what's the exact route - and how do you buy tickets? If it's a cab, do you need exact change? Should you steer clear of certain cab companies? Etc.

- **Download an offline map of your destination area to your phone.** With offline maps, you'll still be able to see your location (the little blue dot) on the map, because your phone will use its inbuilt GPS to figure out where you are.

  - Google Maps allows some countries to be downloaded for offline use - here's a list of them: www.protravel.co/mapsoffline. Here are instructions on how to download a Google Map: www.protravel.co/instructionmaps. There are a few disadvantages to using offline Google Maps though - namely that you can't search for points of interest or get directions to a specific place.

  - If an offline Google Map isn't available for your destination country (or if you want your map to have a bit more functionality), use OsmAnd (www.protravel.co/osmand) - a phone app for offline mapping, which also offers turn-by-turn navigation and an offline point-of-interest database. There are lots of other offline map apps out there, but I always come back to OsmAnd.

- **Learn in advance which SIM card to get for your destination country,** and see if it's possible to buy one at the airport (it often is, and - bonus - the staff at the airport store are more likely to speak English and help you with setting up the card on your phone).

  Register your purchase of this book at www.protravel.co and I'll give you step-by-step instructions for finding the best SIM card in your destination country.

- **At the destination airport, get cash out of the ATM.** In many countries, it's likely you'll need to pay for something in cash before you arrive at your location. (Also, you won't know where the ATMs are near your new home - and the local restaurant you go to on your first night might not accept cards.)

Conclusion

To put this entire chapter and every other grrr thought we have about airports and flying into perspective, we need to remind ourselves - as Louis CK once did - that very soon we'll be "flying through the air like a bird", and "sitting in a chair in the sky". And that's pretty darn cool.

Watch the Louis CK video here: www.protravel.co/skychair.

Conclusion

For a quick summary and useful reference, here are the tips, ideas and strategies that I think have made the biggest difference to my enjoyment of travel and sanity:

- Becoming more minimalist in my approach to packing has probably had the biggest impact on my travelling lifestyle and how free and fulfilled it makes me feel. Read "The benefits of travelling light" (in **Chapter 1: Pack Like A Pro**) for a sense of how great it can be, and all the practical benefits you get when you travel with carry-on baggage only.

- "The Principles of packing" (in **Chapter 1: Pack Like A Pro**) helped me to whittle down my belongings and get out of the habit of needing *everything*, "just in case".

- Skyscanner is still my favourite way to find cheap flights. If you have the time, definitely have a read through of my full instructions on <u>how to find the</u> <u>best-value flights</u> (in **Chapter 2: Book The Best** **Flights**) - it's still pretty quick. If you're really in a rush though, just read the first part: "<u>Start with</u> <u>Skyscanner</u>".

- When it comes to accommodation, Airbnb is always my first port of call. If there are plenty of apartments to choose from at my destination, here's how I whittle them down quickly:

  - First, I "<u>Make use of the map on the search</u> <u>results page</u>" (in **Chapter 3: Find Incredible** **Accommodation**) to make sure I'm only looking at apartments in an area I specifically want to stay in - and to find some gems that are *just* the other side of the border of an expensive area, and therefore much cheaper.

  - I then click on a few of the apartments and use the checklist outlined in "<u>Make sure the</u> <u>apartment has everything you need</u>".

- As for insurance... simply *understanding* how travel insurance and health insurance work was my biggest first step: I had no clue when I first started out! If you're unclear of the differences, read the intros "<u>Travel insurance</u>" and "<u>Expat health insurance</u>" (in

Chapter 4: Suss Out Insurance And Visas).

- Visas are a tricky topic for digital nomads, because our situation doesn't really fall inside the "business visa" or "working visa" category. As a result, most people simply enter a country with a tourist visa (if a visa is needed at all). I use Visa HQ (www.protravel.co/visahq) to find out if I need a tourist visa, then (if I do) I Google around to discover if I can get a visa on arrival or if I should order one in advance. Read more about visas in **Chapter 4: Insurance and Visas**.

- For me, airport survival had a lot to do with being aware of all the airport/airline rules and preparing my gear so that I could sail through check-in, security and the gate. Get up to speed on everything by reading "Know the rules for carry-on baggage" (in **Chapter 5: Survive The Airport**). If you're already aware of all the rules and know how to deal with them, head straight to "Stay organised" for the lowdown on all the ways in which I've saved my marriage over the years. (Even if you're single, I promise they'll come in handy.)

- And finally... register your purchase of this book at www.protravel.co for lots and lots of free stuff that will help you become even more of a travel ninja:

- A walkthrough video to help you find good-value apartments on Airbnb

- Tips on being accepted by an Airbnb host

- A checklist that you MUST follow before you leave for the airport!

- Step-by-step instructions for finding the best SIM card in any country

- **A value-packed bonus chapter called "Settling In"**, with information about local transportation (and how to get to grips with it quickly and easily), finding and making friends with other digital nomads and frequent travellers, learning the language, receiving mail, keeping fit, and SO MUCH MORE!

When it comes to travel websites, travel strategies and travel products, things change frequently: new products, ideas and services are created constantly. The fundamentals never change though - it's all about packing smart, staying organised, and keeping on top of the rules. Now that you have an excellent base level of understanding and a lot of handy links, you should find it pretty easy to keep on top of any changes and apply them to your own travel lifestyle.

I hope I've made all the planning and prep much easier for you, so that you can go on to have a wonderfully exciting onward journey.

Thanks for reading!

Mish

Also by the author…

Protect Your Tech:

Your geek-free guide to a secure and private digital life

If your password for every website is "monkey" or "iloveyou"… you need to read this book.

Learn, in one afternoon, everything you need to know to keep your personal data secure and private when you work, shop and play online - using (mostly) free online tools.

Protect Your Tech is an entertaining, action-oriented guide to safeguarding your digital life. With simple, jargon-free explanations, you'll learn easy steps you can take to keep your personal data safely under wraps.

Buy it on Amazon: <u>www.protravel.co/protectyourtech</u>.

Find out:

- How easy it is for someone to crack your online passwords - even "clever" ones like "Pa55w0rd!"

- The simple, but crucial steps you need to take to protect yourself when you're using your phone or laptop from a cafe, airport or other public place.

- How to make sure that even if your device gets stolen, the thief can't find out anything about you.

- The dangers you're exposed to if you use a "cloud" storage solution like Dropbox or Google Drive - and what to do about it.

- How to avoid getting scammed when you're buying online.

- Much more!

Contains step-by-step instructions for desktop (Windows and Mac) and mobile (iOS and Android) devices.

Buy it on Amazon: <u>www.protravel.co/protectyourtech</u>.

Thank yous

The following people gave me oodles of tips, advice, eyes (well… they proofread the book for me), support and encouragement along the way. Gigantic thanks to you all.

Rob Dix (obvs)

Shayna Oliveira, Christopher Sutton, Nat Sutton, Kelly O'Laughlin, Sabine Pereira, Pete Domican, Anouk Janssens-Bevernage, Holly Kennedy, James Turner, Mark Gibson, Alexander Joo, Lewis Smith, Julie Velky, Lewis Quartey, Lewis Smith, Jenny Smith, Mario Del Duca, Rob Goetting

Appendices

Appendix 1: Travel products and gadgets

In case you want to go on a clicking-and-shopping spree, here are all the items I've mentioned in **Chapter 1: Pack Like A Pro**.

These are all items I use and recommend. If you want to see the items that *other* travellers buy and recommend (with links, of course), just head to www.protravel.co to register your purchase of this book.

Online stores and websites for inspiration

Mostly clothing:

- **Backcountry:** www.protravel.co/backcountry

(international shipping is available)

- **REI:** www.protravel.co/rei (international shipping is available)

- **Icebreaker:** www.protravel.co/icebreaker (international shipping to *some* countries is available)

- **Under Armour:** www.protravel.co/underarmour (international shipping is available)

- **ExOfficio:** www.protravel.co/exofficio (only ships to the US from its online store, but has international retailers - which can be found here: www.protravel.co/exofficio-locator)

- **Amazon:** www.protravel.co/amazon (lots of performance clothing stores also put their products on Amazon)

Mostly gadgets and technology:

- **Eagle Creek:** www.protravel.co/eaglecreek (products are also available on Amazon)

- **Sea To Summit:** www.protravel.co/seatosummit (products are also available on Amazon)

- **Tom Bihn** (accessories page): www.protravel.co/

tbaccessories

- **eBags** (accessories page): www.protravel.co/.
  ebagsaccess

- **humangear**: www.protravel.co/humangear (products
  are also available on Amazon)

- **Kickstarter - technology category:**
  www.protravel.co/kickstarter

- **Outgrow Me**: www.protravel.co/outgrow

- **Too Many Adapters**: www.protravel.co/tma

- **Google** "digital nomad packing list [year]", "travel
  gadgets [year]", "travel tech [year]" etc. for up-to-date
  inspiration and ideas.

Recommended backpacks

- **Tom Bihn Aeronaut 45**: www.protravel.co/aeronaut

- **Tortuga Carry-On Backpack**: www.protravel.co/.
  tortuga

- **Minaal Carry-On Bag**: www.protravel.co/minaal

- **REI Vagabond Tour 40 Pack**: www.protravel.co/

rei40

Go to **Appendix 2** for photos of all these backpacks.

Recommended packing accessories

- **eBags medium packing cube:** www.protravel.co/medcube

- **Eagle Creek Compression Sac:** www.protravel.co/egcompression

- **Flight 001 toiletries bag:** www.protravel.co/flight001

- **Shoe bag:** www.protravel.co/shoebag

- **Tom Bihn Packing Cube Shoulder Bag:** www.protravel.co/shoulderbag

- **Eagle Creek 2-in-1 Waistpack/Shoulder Bag:** www.protravel.co/waistpack

- **Sea to Summit Ultra-Sil Sling Bag:** www.protravel.co/sling

- **Laptop sleeve:** www.protravel.co/laptopsleeve

Recommended gadgets, technology and lightweight items

- **Rab Xenon X Hoodie:** www.protravel.co/rab

- **Panasonic Lumix LX7:** www.protravel.co/lumix

- **Merrell Barefoot Flux Glove:** www.protravel.co/flux

- **X-Mini Portable Capsule Speaker:** www.protravel.co/speaker

- **SanDisk Sansa Clip 8GB:** www.protravel.co/mp3

- **Pacsafe Retractasafe 250 4-Dial Retractable Cable Lock:** www.protravel.co/lock

- **SanDisk Ultra 64GB Memory Card:** www.protravel.co/memory

- **JOBY GorillaPod Flexible Camera Tripod:** www.protravel.co/gorilla

Appendix 2: Backpack photo gallery

Tom Bihn Aeronaut 45

Tortuga Carry-On Backpack

Minaal Carry-On Bag

REI Vagabond Tour 40 Pack

Appendix 3: Travelling with kids and/or pets?

There are plenty of digital nomads and frequent travellers who have kids, pets or both, and - thanks to cheaper flights, better wifi and the compounding effect of *others* doing it - I'm hearing about more and more people who are making "travel" a long-term life plan rather than something to get out of their system while they're young.

While I can't provide advice from personal experience, I can give you links to useful websites and resources from those in the know!

Travelling with kids:

- There are some great podcast interviews with digital nomad families out there. These two in particular are fantastic:

  - Tropical MBA - What is the best place for location independent families? www.protravel.co/tmba1

  - Tropical MBA - How does location independence affect relationships and families? www.protravel.co/tmba2

- Christine Gilbert from Almost Fearless travels with her husband Drew and their two children. She blogs frequently about their experiences as a family as they move around the world: www.protravel.co/almostfearless.

- Jason from An Epic Education writes the most inspirational digital nomad parenting blog I've come across. He's honest, insightful, adventurous and hilarious: www.protravel.co/epiceducation.

- Nomad Forum (www.protravel.co/nomadforum) already has some Q&As about families who travel, but you could also ask your own - most questions get a good level of responses. Here are some questions that have already been asked:

  - What nomads are out there travelling married and/or with a family? www.protravel.co/nomadfamily

  - Is it possible to have children while living a nomadic life? www.protravel.co/nomadchildren

Travelling with pets:

- Pet Travel has useful guides to airline pet policies (www.protravel.co/petairline), pet passports (www.protravel.co/petpassport) and more.

- Christine Gilbert from Almost Fearless has an info-packed blog post on travelling with pets: www.protravel.co/fearlesspets. It's quite an old post - from 2009 - but her points are still relevant.

- Dog Jaunt is a lovely, jam-packed site for anyone who wants to take their dog(s) with them on any sort of trip: www.protravel.co/dogjaunt. It contains destination tips, packing lists, information on paperwork and healthcare, product reviews and lots more.